EZRA POUND

CATHAY

EZRA POUND

CATHAY

THE CENTENNIAL EDITION

Foreword by Mary de Rachewiltz

Edited with an introduction
and
Transcripts of Fenollosa's notes
by Zhaoming Qian

A NEW DIRECTIONS BOOK

Manufactured in the United States of America
First published as a New Directions Paperbook in 2015
Design by Eileen Baumgartner

Library of Congress Cataloging-in-Publication Date
Pound, Ezra, 1885–1972.
[Poems. Selections]
Cathay : the Centennial edition / Ezra Pound ; foreword by Mary de Rachewiltz ; edited with an introduction and transcripts of Fenollosa's notes by Zhaoming Qian. -- First edition.
pages cm
Originally published : London : Mathews, 1915.
Includes bibliographical references and index.
ISBN 978-0-8112-2352-2 (alk. paper)
1. Chinese poetry—Translations into English. I. Fenollosa, Ernest, 1853–1908, writer of added commentary. II. Rachewiltz, Mary de, writer of foreword. III. Qian, Zhaoming, editor, writer of introduction. IV. Pound, Ezra, 1885–1972. Lustra of Ezra Pound. V. Title. VI. Title: Lustra of Ezra Pound.
PS3531.O82A6 2015
811'.54—dc23   2015005787

10 9 8 7 6 5 4

New Directions Books are published for James Laughlin
by New Directions Publishing Corporation
80 Eighth Avenue, New York 10011

Table of Contents

Foreword

by Mary de Rachewiltz

CATHAY: The Lament of the Frontier Guard.

Yes, yes, yes, *in the timeless air:* a new edition of *Cathay* because of its eternal freshness. Good poetry is good currency if kept in circulation, and Zhaoming Qian is the eminently suited editor. Pound would have said: he has done his homework with *Ezra Pound's Chinese Friends* and elsewhere. Together we celebrate Ezra Pound's 130th birthday and pay homage to his friend, Henri Gaudier-Brzeska: *mort pour la patrie* a century ago.

Nearly a century ago T. S. Eliot said: "Pound is the inventor of Chinese poetry for our time." Nowadays one might add a line from the Cantos: "Nor began nor ends anything" (cxiv).

Critics, philologists, scholars have written reams on Pound's translations, his knowing and not knowing Chinese, Fenollosa's misreadings of the ideograms, etc. From the University of Canberra, Igor, my brother-in-law, wrote to me of the Swedish linguist and member of the Academy, Göran Malmqvist—the gist of his lecture seems to be: *malgrè tout,* Ezra Pound's *Cathay* is the best interpretation of Chinese poetry. Dag Hammarsköld, another member of the Swedish Academy, had called Pound "a Seer" and Marie-Noelle Little's *The Knight and the Troubadour* tells the story.

A century ago, a twenty-three-year-old sculptor was writing letters from the trenches: "I'd be glad to see a few Chinese poems," and then, "Many thanks for the poems. I am glad at having the

Rihakus. There is nothing exciting happening." Yet his testament was the VORTEX: "Sculptural energy is the mountain.... VORTEX OF BLACKNESS AND SILENCE: Will and consciousness are our VORTEX." By the time his second installment of "Vortex" was published in *Blast* 2, July 1915, Gaudier-Brzeska, "the most absolute genius," had been killed by a German bullet.

WWI–WWII: When I was the only pupil left in what James Laughlin called the Ezuversity, aged sixteen, walking on the hill-path of Sant'Ambrogio, to exorcise the threats of bombs falling, I was told to translate, as well as some Cantos, "a poem more suited for our time: 'The Lament of the Frontier Guard,'" an ageless anti-war poem, while the poet himself tried to educate, to stop the war, over the air: *radiando* and being most monstrously misunderstood.

In exile, homesick, he had somehow lost touch with "his own kind." The language, by then current among the people of his country, had changed, and though his vision was clear, the Furies ran away with his tongue. Again "a myriad, / And of the best" was being killed. I was given a memoir of *Gaudier-Brzeska* to read (an ND paperback is still in print). A desolate Italian father, Filippo Montanari, sent a slight book of poems by his dead son, Saturno. Pound honored and consoled him by translating them into English. The death of an English aviator poet was recorded in captivity near Pisa: "Angold tethneke" (LVXXXIV).

To assuage sorrow, one of the Poet's "safety valves" was recourse to the classics, memorizing words and lines. In Canto LXXXVIII we read: "The books of a scholar, his countenance (wainagium)."

WWII brought not only the reality of the eternal war, but also new words and rhythms to express it. In the Military Camp at Metato the Poet heard America's new voices. Proof of it is the

Confucian Odes: *The Classic Anthology Defined by Confucius*. Their *tekne* is the best comment on his early translations in *Cathay*.

"The master must have worked hard on the music of the Odes," says Achilles Fang in his introduction in 1954; it applies not only to Confucius but also to Pound. I. A. Richards confirms: "Here is Mr. Pound at his best." The translation had been interrupted, as we know, during the internment in the DTC, but continued as soon as the book was returned and while he was undergoing "treatment" in St. Elizabeths.

Some seeds for a lifelong interest in Chinese poetry, and especially in Confucius, may have unwittingly been sown by Ezra's grandmother, Mary Weston, whose death was the first real "sorrow" recalled, according to Dr. Jerome Kavka. She was an avid reader and the main influence during Pound's childhood. Among her books there is one that has never been mentioned, probably because considered too frivolous: John Kendrick Bangs, *A House-Boat on the Styx, Being some account of the diverse doings of the associated shades* (1895). With the names of numerous ancient philosophers and at the time current characters in the magazine Punch, we find "Members of the House Committee: Walter Raleigh, Demosthenes, Blackstone, Dr. Johnson, Confucius." This may well have been the first encounter with the name of the Chinese Sage.

In 1913 with the Fenollosa windfall of manuscripts came two books, P. Lacharme's *Confucii Chi-King* in Latin, and William Jennings, *The Shi King*. Pound's lifelong study of Chinese poetry, language, and philosophy began. By the time he had finished the Chinese History Cantos, the "Mandate" seemed to be shifting towards America; he completed the John Adams Section and prepared to write his "Paradiso." But people who should be like brothers "because they read the same books" were killing each other and new wars were breaking out, West and East. America closed her doors on her Poet. In March 1941, lines for a new Canto: "birds praising Janequin … clack of bamboos against olive stock" were sent to Japan, but their music was silenced by sheer wrath at the senseless destructions.

By 1958, after revisiting European and Chinese history, his Epic had reached the Naki tribes of Southwest China. In the Pisan Camp Pound remembered that an Australian God took the mouth of his son away because he had made too many words, thereby making clatter. Pound, the "Seer," was "*entmündigt*," the Law took his mouth away, i.e. deprived him of his *Persona Jurídica*. When the consequences of the loss hit him full face, though he still looked physically strong, he felt crushed, exhausted, and we, the young did not realize.

The encounter with his "archive" upon his return to Europe was in many ways a shock, yet he promptly set to work. The Fenollosa material had priority and he clamored, without success, for help. Yet Poetry lives on. Numerous new translations and Chinese anthologies keep appearing. In *Confucius to Cummings* we find versions from the 1954 Odes and *Cathay*. The comparison and the choice of the texts speak for themselves. Rihaku's "Exile's Letter" sums up the overall tenderness of the 1915 edition: a young girl's longing, the sadness of a beautiful woman left too much alone, and above all the parting of friends, separations, leave-taking. In Italy in 1958 to commemorate the fiftieth anniversary of Fenollosa's death, Vanni Scheiwiller was encouraged to bring out my translation of *Cathay* in a bilingual, English-Italian edition. His father, Giovanni, had published *Kung Fu Tsu* in his newly founded "Pesce d'Oro" series in 1937 and in his honor Pound translated "By the River of Stars," recapturing the delicacy of his early vein. The poem was included, with previously unpublished notes, in the 1987 bilingual edition. In 1989 Andrea Molesini included a new version of *Cathay* in his *La Muraglia Infinita*. In 1993 Einaudi published *Antiche Poesie Cinesi*, the original Chinese text translated by Alessandra C. Lavagnino and Maria Rita Masci with Pound's English text and my Italian. In short, *Cathay* is being kept in circulation.

Actually, a minted "copper coin" with Jefferson on one side and Pound on the other, un *soldo contro i soldi*, was inserted on the last page of Tonino Guerra's edition of *L'Albero dell'Acqua*, Scheiwiller 1992, with an introduction by Luca Cesari. The innumerable ramifications and meetings of rivers as well as generations of poets, their languages and dialects continue along with "life's little ironies": Guerra means War. Tonino, poet and screenwriter, born in Sant'Arcangelo in Romagna, after the concentration camp in Germany, planted a garden of "forgotten fruits" laid out carpet/monuments to Dante and Pound under the tower of Bascio in Pennabilli and translated into Romagnolo dialect "Lament of the Frontier Guard": *Lamento di Una Guardia di Frontiera*, Libri Scheiwiller, 2000.

CATHAY: Poems by Ezra Pound. A short film by Bernard Dew was shown on September 1, 2002, at the Sala Volpi in Venice.

Introduction

On December 18, 1914, Henri Gaudier-Brzeska wrote from the trenches near the Marne to Ezra Pound in London, linking the latter's manuscript poems to his fellow soldiers' case: "The poems depict our situation in a wonderful way. We do not yet eat the young nor old fern shoots, but we cannot be over victualled where we stand." Three-and-a-half months later, in April 1915, the poems the soon-to-be-killed French sculptor found appropriate to his World War I experience were published along with others in an edition of 1,000 copies by Elkin Matthews of London under the title *Cathay*.

* * *

Since its first publication in 1915, *Cathay* has been read both as a translation and as original poetry. Pound himself wanted *Cathay* to be read as a translation, having consistently retained the original subtitle—TRANSLATIONS BY EZRA POUND FOR THE MOST PART FROM THE CHINESE OF RIHAKU, FROM THE NOTES OF THE LATE ERNEST FENOLLOSA, AND THE DECIPHERINGS OF THE PROFESSORS MORI AND ARIGA—but it is equally appropriate to read *Cathay* as original poetry. One proof that Pound designed it as such is his inclusion of "The Seafarer" in the first printing. In 1914, speaking of his 1911 "Seafarer" and the *Cathay* poems, Pound explained, "I began this search for the real in a book called *Personae*, casting off, as it were, complete masks of the self in each poem. I continued in long series of translations, which were but more elaborate masks." In 1916, *Cathay* was reprinted in *Lustra* without "The Seafarer" and with four more Chinese poems based on the notes of Ernest Fenollosa (1853–1908), a Harvard-trained scholar, who spent fifteen years in Japan (1878–90 and 1897–1901) teaching Western philosophy and studying Eastern art and poetry. These added Chinese poems in *Lustra* were included in *Personae* (1926) and *Selected Poems of Ezra Pound* (1928). The omission of the Anglo-Saxon piece in all the versions of *Cathay* since *Lustra* has somewhat obscured Pound's original dual purpose. *[precision of imagery]*

Pound's writing of *Cathay* coincided with his Imagist and Vorticist campaigns. He first experimented with a concise, lucid style in *Ripostes* (1912) and four Chinese adaptations from Herbert Giles—his contributions to the anthology he edited, *Des Imagistes* (1914). Indeed, it was the concise, graphic qualities of poems like "In a Station of the Metro" that convinced Fenollosa's widow, Mary Fenollosa, to choose Pound as her late husband's literary executor. After meeting Pound in the fall of 1913, she sent him "Fenollosa's treasures," permitting him to make out of them a Chinese poetry anthology, a Japanese Noh drama anthology, and an essay on the Chinese character. In Fenollosa's Chinese poetry materials, Pound discovered a new model that at once mirrored and challenged his developing poetics. As he makes clear in his 1918 essay on "Chinese Poetry," he translated Chinese poetry precisely because it "has certain qualities of vivid presentation." For Pound, poetry's visual aspect, or phanopoeia, can be translated without much difficulty, whereas poetry's musical effect, or melopoeia, is hardly translatable. Accordingly, in selecting poems for *Cathay*, Pound kept only those that shared his Imagist/Vorticist sensibilities and in recreating them he focused almost entirely on their "vivid presentation." As a result, despite numerous deviations (accidental or intentional), Pound succeeds in recapturing the poems' overall sense and sentiment,

[cubism harsh,angular]

disregarding their "rhymes" and "tones" while following their verbal constructions and methods of presentation.

As a translation *Cathay* has been criticized as well as admired. Because of the huge impact Pound made on Chinese translation, T. S. Eliot famously called him "the inventor of Chinese poetry for our time." Indeed, *Cathay* was the first book to effectively introduce classical Chinese poets to a twentieth-century English-reading public. The work's harshest criticisms have come from sinologists, who have good reason to question Pound's qualifications as a Chinese translator. A fluent reader of seven Western languages, Pound did not know a word of Chinese at the time. His fellow American co-translator, Fenollosa, on the other hand, had to depend on Professor Mori and other Japanese tutors to interpret the poems of Li Bai ("Rihaku") and other Chinese masters. Fenollosa's autograph notes that record Chinese poetry sessions with Mori and others in Tokyo, from 1897 to 1901, are notoriously messy. Not surprisingly, Pound was led to conflate two separate Li Bai poems into "The River Song." Without consulting the Fenollosa notes, anyone is likely to blame Pound for all the misrepresentations. In 1969, the poet and scholar Wai-lim Yip made a pioneering effort to examine *Cathay*'s complex relation with the Fenollosa notes and the Chinese originals. He sought to ascertain where Pound was responsible for a deviation, where he was misled by Fenollosa/Mori, and where he penetrated through the surface of Fenollosa's shorthand glosses to the original meaning. Take "The River-Merchant's Wife: A Letter," for example. Pound has been ridiculed for presenting a line meaning "You came by on a bamboo stick horse" as "You came by on bamboo stilts, playing horse," and another line suggesting that "It is impossible to traverse in the fifth month" as "And you have been gone five months." While the latter distortion was Pound's, the former was derived from Fenollosa's faulty gloss ("bamboo stilts"). Wai-lim Yip's "triple comparison" has also helped reveal Pound's gift for occasionally catching original meanings from the context and repairing his co-translators' inaccuracies. In his notes for a line in "Exile's Letter," for instance, Fenollosa improperly introduces the first-person singular pronoun "I" into a context where agents are absent: "(And) once drunk for months together I despised Kings & princes." By replacing "I" with "we"—changing Fenollosa's crib to "And we were drunk for month on month, forgetting the kings and princes"—Pound succeeds in restoring the integrity of that line and of the entire poem, for the poem's keynote is nostalgia for a lost poetic community, which was muddled by Fenollosa's insertion of the pronoun "I."

Ironically, it is for other reasons, generally, that *Cathay* has been praised as a superb translation. Pound's resistance to his own former archaism and to late Victorian poetic conventions appeals especially to twentieth-century readers. Among the few who had translated Chinese poetry into English before *Cathay* was a British diplomat in China named Herbert Giles. Pound abhorred his late Victorian style and the target language he used, which erased virtually all Chinese cultural codes. In adapting four of Giles' Chinese poems, he stripped away their irrelevant English meter, rhyme, and stanzaic pattern. One of them, a poem with "thee" and "thou" in pentameter, was a version of a Han-dynasty ballad. In it Pound discerned the equation of a court lady's fate with that of a silk fan. In his adaptation, "Fan-Piece, for Her Imperial Lord," he managed to intensify the poem's emotional energy within three unadorned suggestive lines: "O fan of white silk, / clear as frost on the grass-blade, / You also are laid aside." At the time Pound regarded translation as a re-creation of a foreign text into the present-day English idiom. Pound's pre-Fenollosan Chinese adaptions paved the way for *Cathay*. Compared with the language of the Chinese translations by Herbert Giles, W.A.P. Martin, and so on, the verbal constructions of *Cathay*, like those of Pound's earlier Chinese adaptations, are distinctly colloquial and contemporary.

To what extent did Pound succeed in transmitting the Chinese originals' cultural values and aesthetic merits? Pound's manipulations surely affected the originals' qualities. With a mind to intensify antiwar emotion, Pound in "Song of the Bowmen of Shu" goes so far as to reinvent a line meaning "four horses are tied" as "his horses are tired." To ensure easy reading, he has the speaker of "The River-Merchant's Wife" say "Forever and forever, and forever," where Li Bai's river-merchant's wife actually utters a line alluding to a legendary figure who allowed himself to be drowned holding onto a pillar under a bridge waiting for his lover. Have such Poundian interferences diminished the so-called "Chineseness" of the originals?

While the Poundian line "his horses are tired" is an extreme case of aggressive meddling, examples of turning Chinese allusions into passages in conformity with the culture of the English-speaking world can be found everywhere in *Cathay*. The final section of "Poem by the Bridge at Ten-Shin" alone alludes to three historical figures. The first, Li Si, "a favorite" of the First Emperor of China, as Fenollosa notes, "did not retire with death of [the First] Emperor," and the Second Emperor of China chose to have him executed. Seeing his yellow dog on his way to execution, he lamented to his son: "Pleasant were the days when we hunted with that dog!" The second figure, "the lady Riokushu," was a beautiful woman, who brought animosity to her husband and death to herself. The last, "Han-rei" or Fan Li, was a strategist, who relinquished power upon completion of his task to defeat his king's rival. It is true that the relevant lines are stripped of the figures' stories, but from the context readers can easily discern their moral stature. In the first case, "yellow dogs' howl" signals an end to the pleasures of the powerful men and women described above. Additionally, the lady Riokushu is a femme fatale; and "Han-rei," departing "alone with his mistress," acts as a foil to the others.

Unlike T. S. Eliot and Marianne Moore, Pound is not in the habit of providing footnotes for his readers. His heavily allusive poetry relies on the context, immediate or remote, for comprehension. Does Pound's tendency to assimilate Chinese allusions to his own culture imply a bias against the strategy of retaining foreign elements in translation? Pound has his own strategy to preserve what is foreign in translation. In the passage above, he preserves foreign proper names, "the lady Riokushu" and "Han-rei," to hint at concealed cross-cultural information. Use of foreign proper names—Pound's way to ensure what Marcel Duchamp calls "maximum precision" and what Marjorie Perloff calls the "infra-thin difference between . . . objects from the same mold"—gives Pound's works their curious authenticity, their sense of being there. Foreign proper names abound in *Cathay* as well as in Pound's other works. Thus, in "The River-Merchant's Wife," the couple grew up together in "the village of Chokan," and when the husband "went into far Ku-to-Yen," the wife would like to meet him "As far as Cho-fu-Sa." Why does Pound prefer naming the port Fenollosa glosses "Long Wind Sand" "Cho-fu-Sa"? Why does he fill *Cathay* with Japanese-sounding Chinese proper names? An obvious reason is to strike a balance between the familiar and the strange.

Pound's ignorance of the Chinese language in the 1910s should not suggest that he had no knowledge of China at the time. Before *Cathay*, around 1909 to 1912, Pound made frequent visits to the British Museum's collection of Chinese art. The Chinese art objects that had impressed his eye could serve as a guide, clarifying images and situations in Fenollosa's Chinese materials. The opening line of "The River-Merchant's Wife" has been celebrated for its effect—in contrast to W.A.P. Martin's not at all foreign "My head a mass of curls"—precisely because in presenting the little girl's hairstyle, Pound relies not on Fenollosa's scholarship but on his common sense enlightened by classical Chinese painting. "Taking Leave of a Friend" reveals another example of this in connection to the phrase *hui shou* as a farewell gesture. Fenollosa and Mori gloss it as "Shaking hands" or "Brandishing [hands]." In modern China, the expression means "wave raised hand(s)." Li Bai's contemporaries, however, would bow over clasped hands to greet each other and wave clasped hands in front of the chest at parting. Could they bow over clasped hands at parting? They could when taking leave of a valued friend, something Pound could have seen in an old Chinese picture. His foreignized "bow over their clasped hands" is therefore not culturally incorrect.

* * *

Cathay was put together by Pound according to Mori's description of certain classical Chinese anthologies: "more 'creative' than 'creating anew.'" Since its inclusion in *Personae* (1926), the sequence has been accepted as original Pound work. Ford Madox Ford, who had laughed at Pound's archaism in *Canzoni* (1911) to the point of falling over and rolling about on the floor was in 1915 so dazzled by the freshness and simplicity of *Cathay* that he applauded: "If these are original verses, then Mr. Pound is the greatest poet of this day." Eliot, who quotes the above comment in *Ezra Pound: His Metric and Poetry*, also quotes Ford as observing, "The poems in 'Cathay' are things of a supreme beauty," to which he adds, "'Cathay' will, I believe, rank with the 'Sea-Farer' in the future among Mr. Pound's original work."

The special appeal of *Cathay* resides in its language modeled on contemporary Anglo-American speech—concise, lucid, and "as well written as prose"—as well as in a kind of "otherness" of content and presentation. As Pound remarks on Chinese taste, "the Chinese *like* poetry that they have to think about, and even poetry that they have to puzzle over." The four short lines of "The Jewel Stairs' Grievance," for instance, might not make much sense to any Westerner at one reading, "[y]et upon careful examination," Pound declares, "we find that everything is there, not merely by 'suggestion' but by a sort of mathematical process of reduction."

For Pound a good poet should "fill his mind with the finest cadences he can discover, preferably in a foreign language." And he follows his own advice in *Cathay* in mimicking hardly translatable Chinese melopoeia. One example is "The Beautiful Toilet." In the original, each of the first six lines begins with the repetition of a word. Such repetition would sound too heavy-handed in English, so instead Pound mimics the original's repetition only in the first and fourth lines ("Blue, blue . . ."; "White, white . . ."), turning repetition of words to pairings of sounds in the second and third lines ("And the wi*ll*ows have over*fill*ed . . ." and "And w*i*th*i*n, the m*i*stress, *i*n the m*i*dm*o*st . . ."), and setting the repeated words apart in the fifth line ("Slender, she puts forth a slender hand").

Imitations of Chinese melopoeis, found also in "To-Em-Mei's 'The Unmoving Cloud" ("The clouds have gathered, and gathered" and "Rain, rain, and the clouds have gathered"), are more often appreciated by readers as original creations. There are traces of

Cathay's experiments with repetition in Pound's modernist epic *The Cantos:* "Ear, ear for the sea-surge, murmur of old men's voices . . . Evil and further evil, and a curse cursed on our children"(Canto 2). Syntactically awkward juxtapositions such as "Beat, beat, whirr, thud, in the soft turf" (Canto 4) and "Rain; empty river; a voyage" (Canto 49) can likewise be attributed to Pound's encounter with classical Chinese poetry.

Pound was from the beginning an allusive poet. It was Fenollosa's notes, however, that enabled him to add a Chinese element to his multiple allusions—Greek, Latin, Provençal, modern European, or American. From Chinese poets Pound learned to nominalize elusive concepts and morals. His typical technique is to set a foreign proper name in the line right above its allusive idea in English— "the lady Riokushu" on top of "cause of hate," and "Ku-to-Yen" on top of "far" and "by the river of swirling eddies." Pound detested abstractions. In *The Cantos*, Chinese proper names frequently occur in conjunction with Western proper names to illuminate abstract concepts. His aim is to convey a "sense of being there"while getting his idea across. An example is in the opening section of Canto 85, where the Chinese character 靈 (LING²)is set right above I Yin ("All roots by the time of I Yin"), "Galilio index'd 1616,""Wellington's peace after Vaterloo," Queen Bess who "translated Ovid," and Cleopatra, who "wrote of the currency." From Canto 78 one learns that Tching Tang was wise in choosing I Yin to run his country: "Chose I Yin and the crooks toddled off." The character 靈, "a great sensitivity" according to Pound, takes on wider meanings when it is juxtaposed with relevant proper names, which in turn are juxtaposed with relevant events and anecdotes. For Pound proper names, Chinese or otherwise, are "the poet's pigment"; they are "lords over fact, over race-long recurrent moods, and over to-morrow."

To see Imagism/Vorticism at work, one should read *Cathay*'s centerpiece "Exile's Letter," which Pound designated in 1920, along with "The Seafarer" and "Homage to Sextus Propertius," as one of his "major personae." Here Pound is at his best as a Vorticist. When his speaker is enraptured, readers participate in his Vorticist visions. When his speaker is brought to isolation, readers share his Vortex-like confusion. As the poem comes to its end, the reader hears the voice of "a broken man, speaking . . . an apology for speaking at all": "What is the use of talking, and there is no end of talking, / There is no end of things in the heart." This voice echoes those of lone women in "The Beautiful Toilet," "The River-Merchant's Wife," and "The Jewel Stairs' Grievance," of somber soldiers in "Song of the Bowmen of Shu," "Lament of the Frontier Guard," and "South-Folk in Cold Country," and of solitary poets in "Four Poems of Departure" and "The Unmoving Cloud." This voice also echoes that of the Anglo-Saxon "Seafarer." This distinct Poundian voice indeed unites the *Cathay* poems into a coherent whole.

To read *Cathay* is to contemplate transpacific exchange in Pound's creative work. It is to be aware of transnationalism and transculturalism within American literature. In a globalized age it seems less and less justified to read American literature in isolation from the rest of the world. Within American literature are worlds beyond the borders of the U.S. and across the Atlantic, the Pacific, and the Americas.

* * *

This centennial edition of *Cathay* reproduces for the first time in a century the text of the original 1915 publication in a single volume, plus the poems "Sennin Poem by Kakuhaku," "A Ballad of the Mulberry Road," "Old Idea of Choan by Rosoriu," and "To-Em-Mei's 'The Unmoving Cloud,'" from *Lustra* (1916), along with my transcripts of all the relevant Fenollosa notes. My transcripts are based on a careful examination of the original Fenollosa notebooks archived at the Beinecke Library of Yale University as well as the transcripts of Fenollosa's notes for eight of the *Cathay* poems prepared and published by Hugh Kenner (1971), Sanehide Kodama (1984), and Ronald Bush with George Bornstein (1985). In *Cathay* (1915), Pound ascribes "Song of the Bowmen of Shu," "The Beautiful Toilet," and the epigraph to "Four Poems of Departure" to the wrong poets. The acknowledged sources of "Song of the Bowmen of Shu" and "The Beautiful Toilet" and the poet of the epigraph are given in square brackets in my transcripts of Fenollosa's notes for these poems. Fenollosa's notes for "Song of the Bowmen of Shu," "The Beautiful Toilet," "Sennin Poem by Kakuhaku," and "A Ballad of the Mulberry Road" contain the corresponding Chinese texts. In my transcripts, I have inserted in square brackets the *Quan Tang Shi* and *Tao Yuanming Ji* Chinese texts for the rest of the poems. Inserted in square brackets is also the pinyin romanization for the Chinese. Glaring errors in the Fenollosa notes I have corrected in my footnotes.

My greatest debt is to Mary de Rachewiltz, who provided crucial encouragement. I am grateful to Barry Ahearn, George Bornstein, and Ronald Bush for their helpful suggestions. I would like to thank Tao He, Ying Kong, Hong Ou, Rong Ou, and Zuoyan Yin for their responses to my inquiries. I would like to acknowledge as well the staff of the Beinecke Library at Yale University for their assistance. Thanks must also go to my editors Jeffrey Yang and Declan Spring, whose passion for poetry proved to be an inspiration. As always, I am indebted to my wife May for her support.

—ZHAOMING QIAN

(chou)

"Shu" dynasty arose and Bunno
was esteemed as a Saint.

采薇采薇。 薇亦作止*

Sai, bi, sai, bi,　　 bi, eki, saku, shi,
to pick off, a kind of edible fern,　 also to grow.

We pick off the "Warabi" which
first grow from the earth.

* The letter 止 is no meaning,
no use, but each phrase being
composed of 4 letters, this is
put at the last of phrase.

曰歸曰歸。 歲亦莫止

eten, ki, eten, ki.　 sai, eki, ~~baku~~, shi,
to say, to return,　　 year, also, come to last.

We say to each other " when will
we return to our country?"

CATHAY

TRANSLATIONS BY

EZRA POUND

FOR THE MOST PART FROM THE CHINESE
OF RIHAKU, FROM THE NOTES OF THE
LATE ERNEST FENOLLOSA, AND
THE DECIPHERINGS OF THE
PROFESSORS MORI
AND ARIGA

RIHAKU flourished in the eighth century of our era. The Anglo-Saxon Seafarer is of about this period. The other poems from the Chinese are earlier.

Song of the Bowmen of Shu

[handwritten: signaling change in season,]

HERE we are, picking the first fern-shoots *[handwritten: → spring]*
And saying: When shall we get back to our
    country?
Here we are because we have the Ken-nin for our
    foemen,
We have no comfort because of these Mongols.
We grub the soft fern-shoots,
When anyone says "Return," the others are full of
    sorrow.
Sorrowful minds, sorrow is strong, we are hungry
    and thirsty.
Our defence is not yet made sure, no one can let
    his friend return.
We grub the old fern-stalks. *[handwritten: → shift from soft to old]*
We say: Will we be let to go back in October?
There is no ease in royal affairs, we have no comfort.
Our sorrow is bitter, but we would not return to our
    country.
What flower has come into blossom? *[handwritten: theme: longing for home, fighting for a cause you don't believe in]*
Whose chariot? The General's. *[handwritten: → nod to power structure]*
Horses, his horses even, are tired. They were strong.

Song of the Bowmen of Shu

We have no rest, three battles a month.
By heaven, his horses are tired.
The generals are on them, the soldiers are by them.
The horses are well trained, the generals have ivory
    arrows and quivers ornamented with fish-
    skin.
The enemy is swift, we must be careful.
When we set out, the willows were drooping with
    spring,
We come back in the snow,
We go slowly, we are hungry and thirsty,
Our mind is full of sorrow, who will know of our
    grief?

By Kutsugen.
4th Century B.C.

[handwritten annotations: "more focused around the horses"; "a sense of powerlessness"]

The Beautiful Toilet

[handwritten: → Why toilet ?]

BLUE, blue is the grass about the river
And the willows have overfilled the close garden.
And within, the mistress, in the midmost of her
    youth,
White, white of face, hesitates, passing the door.
Slender, she puts forth a slender hand,

And she was a courtezan in the old days,
And she has married a sot,
Who now goes drunkenly out
And leaves her too much alone.

By Mei Sheng.
B.C. 140.

[handwritten: beauty of nature]
[handwritten: beauty of the woman]
[handwritten: misfortune of the woman]

29

poem of departure

The River Song

lots of vivid imagery

THIS boat is of shato-wood, and its gunwales are
  cut magnolia,
Musicians with jewelled flutes and with pipes of gold
Fill full the sides in rows, and our wine
Is rich for a thousand cups.
We carry singing girls, drift with the drifting water,
Yet Sennin needs
A yellow stork for a charger, and all our seamen
Would follow the white gulls or ride them.

proper names bring the foreign element

Kutsu's prose song
Hangs with the sun and moon.

song goes up

King So's terraced palace
                is now but barren hill,
But I draw pen on this barge
Causing the five peaks to tremble,
And I have joy in these words
                like the joy of blue islands.
(If glory could last forever
Then the waters of Han would flow northward.)

↳ fleeting nature of fortune

against nature's way, glory cannot last forever

* hierarchy of social order

* nature in the sun, moon, blue islands

indexical →

30

The River Song

And I have moped in the Emperor's garden, await-
    ing an order-to-write !
I looked at the dragon-pond, with its willow-
    coloured water
Just reflecting the sky's tinge,
And heard the five-score nightingales aimlessly
    singing.

{ more imagery

The eastern wind brings the green colour into the
    island grasses at Yei-shu,
The purple house and the crimson are full of Spring
    softness.
South of the pond the willow-tips are half-blue and
    bluer,
Their cords tangle in mist, against the brocade-like
    palace.
Vine-strings a hundred feet long hang down from
    carved railings,
And high over the willows, the fine birds sing to
    each other, and listen,
Crying—'Kwan, Kuan,' for the early wind, and the
    feel of it.
The wind bundles itself into a bluish cloud and
    wanders off.
Over a thousand gates, over a thousand doors are
    the sounds of spring singing,

this version is overwhelmed w/ imagery

31

The River Song

And the Emperor is at Ko.
Five clouds hang aloft, bright on the purple sky,
The imperial guards come forth from the golden
      house with their armour a-gleaming.
The emperor in his jewelled car goes out to inspect
      his flowers,
He goes out to Hori, to look at the wing-flapping
      storks,
He returns by way of Sei rock, to hear the new
      nightingales,
For the gardens at Jo-run are full of new nightin-
  gales,
Their sound is mixed in this flute,
Their voice is in the twelve pipes here.

By Rihaku.
8th century A.D.

[handwritten note: new? change has occured]

The River-Merchant's Wife: a Letter

WHILE my hair was still cut straight across my
        forehead
I played about the front gate, pulling flowers.
You came by on bamboo stilts, playing horse,
You walked about my seat, playing with blue plums.
And we went on living in the village of Chokan:
Two small people, without dislike or suspicion.

At fourteen I married My Lord you.
I never laughed, being bashful.
Lowering my head, I looked at the wall.
Called to, a thousand times, I never looked back.

At fifteen I stopped scowling,
I desired my dust to be mingled with yours
Forever and forever, and forever.
Why should I climb the look out?

At sixteen you departed,
You went into far Ku-to-Yen, by the river of swirl-
        ing eddies,

The River-Merchant's Wife: a Letter

And you have been gone five months.
The monkeys make sorrowful noise overhead.
You dragged your feet when you went out.
By the gate now, the moss is grown, the different
      mosses,
Too deep to clear them away!
The leaves fall early this autumn, in wind.
The paired butterflies are already yellow with
      August
Over the grass in the West garden,
They hurt me,
I grow older,
If you are coming down through the narrows of the
      river Kiang,
Please let me know beforehand,
And I will come out to meet you,
      As far as Cho-fu-Sa.
        By Rihaku.

The Jewel Stairs' Grievance

THE jewelled steps are already quite white with
      dew,
It is so late that the dew soaks my gauze stockings,
And I let down the crystal curtain
And watch the moon through the clear autumn.

                                    By Rihaku.

NOTE—Jewel stairs, therefore a palace. Grievance, there-
fore there is something to complain of. Gauze stockings,
therefore a court lady, not a servant who complains. Clear
autumn, therefore he has no excuse on account of the weather.
Also she has come early, for the dew has not merely whitened
the stairs, but has soaked her stockings. The poem is espe-
cially prized because she utters no direct reproach.

Poem by the Bridge at Ten-Shin

MARCH has come to the bridge head,
Peach boughs and apricot boughs hang over a
      thousand gates,
At morning there are flowers to cut the heart,
And evening drives them on the eastward-flowing
      waters.
Petals are on the gone waters and on the going,
    And on the back-swirling eddies,
But to-day's men are not the men of the old days,
Though they hang in the same way over the bridge-
      rail.

The sea's colour moves at the dawn
And the princes still stand in rows, about the throne,
And the moon falls over the portals of Sei-go-yo,
And clings to the walls and the gate-top.
With head-gear glittering against the cloud and
        sun,
The lords go forth from the court, and into far
      borders.
They ride upon dragon-like horses,

Poem by the Bridge at Ten-Shin

Upon horses with head-trappings of yellow-metal,
And the streets make way for their passage.
                    Haughty their passing,
Haughty their steps as they go into great banquets,
To high halls and curious food,
To the perfumed air and girls dancing,
To clear flutes and clear singing;
To the dance of the seventy couples;
To the mad chase through the gardens.
Night and day are given over to pleasure
And they think it will last a thousand autumns,
                    Unwearying autumns.
For them the yellow dogs howl portents in vain,
And what are they compared to the Lady Riokushu,
                    That was cause of hate!
Who among them is a man like Han-rei
          Who departed alone with his mistress,
With her hair unbound, and he his own skiffs-man!
                              By Rihaku.

Lament of the Frontier Guard

By the North Gate, the wind blows full of sand,
Lonely from the beginning of time until now!
Trees fall, the grass goes yellow with autumn.
I climb the towers and towers
                    to watch out the barbarous land:
Desolate castle, the sky, the wide desert.
There is no wall left to this village.
Bones white with a thousand frosts,
High heaps, covered with trees and grass;
Who brought this to pass?
Who has brought the flaming imperial anger?
Who has brought the army with drums and with
                    kettle-drums?
Barbarous kings.
A gracious spring, turned to blood-ravenous autumn,
A turmoil of wars-men, spread over the middle
                    kingdom,
Three hundred and sixty thousand,
And sorrow, sorrow like rain.
Sorrow to go, and sorrow, sorrow returning,
Desolate, desolate fields,

Lament of the Frontier Guard

And no children of warfare upon them,
    No longer the men for offence and defence.
Ah, how shall you know the dreary sorrow at the
    North Gate,
With Rihoku's name forgotten,
And we guardsmen fed to the tigers.
                  Rihaku.

Exile's Letter

To So-Kin of Rakuyo, ancient friend, Chancellor
    of Gen.
Now I remember that you built me a special tavern
By the south side of the bridge at Ten-Shin.
With yellow gold and white jewels, we paid for
    songs and laughter
And we were drunk for month on month, forget-
    ting the kings and princes.
Intelligent men came drifting in from the sea and
    from the west border,
And with them, and with you especially
There was nothing at cross purpose,
And they made nothing of sea-crossing or of
    mountain crossing,
If only they could be of that fellowship,
And we all spoke out our hearts and minds, and
    without regret.

And then I was sent off to South Wei,
        smothered in laurel groves,
And you to the north of Raku-hoku,

Till we had nothing but thoughts and memories in
    common.

And then, when separation had come to its worst,
We met, and travelled into Sen-Go,
Through all the thirty-six folds of the turning and
    twisting waters,
Into a valley of the thousand bright flowers,
That was the first valley;
And into ten thousand valleys full of voices and
    pine-winds.
And with silver harness and reins of gold,
Out come the East of Kan foreman and his
    company.
And there came also the "True man" of Shi-yo to
    meet me,
Playing on a jewelled mouth-organ.
In the storied houses of San-Ko they gave us more
    Sennin music,
Many instruments, like the sound of young phœnix
    broods.
The foreman of Kan Chu, drunk, danced
        because his long sleeves wouldn't keep still
With that music-playing.
And I, wrapped in brocade, went to sleep with my
    head on his lap,

And my spirit so high it was all over the heavens,
And before the end of the day we were scattered
      like stars, or rain.
I had to be off to So, far away over the waters,
You back to your river-bridge.

And your father, who was brave as a leopard,
Was governor in Hei Shu, and put down the bar-
      barian rabble.
And one May he had you send for me,
          despite the long distance.
And what with broken wheels and so on, I won't
      say it wasn't hard going,
Over roads twisted like sheeps' guts.
And I was still going, late in the year,
          in the cutting wind from the North,
And thinking how little you cared for the cost,
          and you caring enough to pay it.
And what a reception:
Red jade cups, food well set on a blue jewelled table,
And I was drunk, and had no thought of returning.
And you would walk out with me to the western
      corner of the castle,
To the dynastic temple, with water about it clear
      as blue jade,

With boats floating, and the sound of mouth-
      organs and drums,
With ripples like dragon-scales, going grass green
      on the water,
Pleasure lasting, with courtezans, going and coming
      without hindrance,
With the willow-flakes falling like snow,
And the vermilioned girls getting drunk about
      sunset,
And the water a hundred feet deep reflecting green
      eyebrows
—Eyebrows painted green are a fine sight in young
      moonlight,
Gracefully painted—
And the girls singing back at each other,
Dancing in transparent brocade,
And the wind lifting the song, and interrupting it,
Tossing it up under the clouds.
           And all this comes to an end.
           And is not again to be met with.
I went up to the court for examination,
Tried Layu's luck, offered the Choyu song,
And got no promotion,
          and went back to the East Mountains
          white-headed.

And once again, later, we met at the South bridge-
    head.
And then the crowd broke up, you went north to
    San palace,
And if you ask how I regret that parting:
    It is like the flowers falling at Spring's end
        Confused, whirled in a tangle.
What is the use of talking, and there is no end of
    talking,
There is no end of things in the heart.

I call in the boy,
Have him sit on his knees here
        To seal this,
And send it a thousand miles, thinking.

                    By Rihaku.

The Seafarer

(*From the early Anglo-Saxon text*)

MAY I for my own self song's truth reckon,
Journey's jargon, how I in harsh days
Hardship endured oft.
Bitter breast-cares have I abided,
Known on my keel many a care's hold,
And dire sea-surge, and there I oft spent
Narrow nightwatch nigh the ship's head
While she tossed close to cliffs. Coldly afflicted,
My feet were by frost benumbed.
Chill its chains are; chafing sighs
Hew my heart round and hunger begot
Mere-weary mood. Lest man know not
That he on dry land loveliest liveth,
List how I, care-wretched, on ice-cold sea,
Weathered the winter, wretched outcast
Deprived of my kinsmen;
Hung with hard ice-flakes, where hail-scur flew,
There I heard naught save the harsh sea
And ice-cold wave, at whiles the swan cries,
Did for my games the gannet's clamour,

The Seafarer

Sea-fowls' loudness was for me laughter,
The mews' singing all my mead-drink.
Storms, on the stone-cliffs beaten, fell on the stern
In icy feathers; full oft the eagle screamed
With spray on his pinion.
                      Not any protector
May make merry man faring needy.
This he little believes, who aye in winsome life
Abides 'mid burghers some heavy business,
Wealthy and wine-flushed, how I weary oft
Must bide above brine.
Neareth nightshade, snoweth from north,
Frost froze the land, hail fell on earth then
Corn of the coldest. Nathless there knocketh now
The heart's thought that I on high streams
The salt-wavy tumult traverse alone.
Moaneth alway my mind's lust
That I fare forth, that I afar hence
Seek out a foreign fastness.
For this there's no mood-lofty man over earth's
        midst,
Not though he be given his good, but will have in
        his youth greed;
Nor his deed to the daring, nor his king to the
        faithful
But shall have his sorrow for sea-fare

The Seafarer

Whatever his lord will.
He hath not heart for harping, nor in ring-having
Nor winsomeness to wife, nor world's delight
Nor any whit else save the wave's slash,
Yet longing comes upon him to fare forth on the
      water.
Bosque taketh blossom, cometh beauty of berries,
Fields to fairness, land fares brisker,
All this admonisheth man eager of mood,
The heart turns to travel so that he then thinks
On flood-ways to be far departing.
Cuckoo calleth with gloomy crying,
He singeth summerward, bodeth sorrow,
The bitter heart's blood. Burgher knows not—
He the prosperous man—what some perform
Where wandering them widest draweth.
So that but now my heart burst from my breast-
      lock,
My mood 'mid the mere-flood,
Over the whale's acre, would wander wide.
On earth's shelter cometh oft to me,
Eager and ready, the crying lone-flyer,
Whets for the whale-path the heart irresistibly,
O'er tracks of ocean; seeing that anyhow
My lord deems to me this dead life
On loan and on land, I believe not

The Seafarer

That any earth-weal eternal standeth
Save there be somewhat calamitous
That, ere a man's tide go, turn it to twain.
Disease or oldness or sword-hate
Beats out the breath from doom-gripped body.
And for this, every earl whatever, for those speak-
      ing after–
Laud of the living, boasteth some last word,
That he will work ere he pass onward,
Frame on the fair earth 'gainst foes his malice,
Daring ado, . . .
So that all men shall honour him after
And his laud beyond them remain 'mid the English,
Aye, for ever, a lasting life's-blast,
Delight mid the doughty.
                  Days little durable,
And all arrogance of earthen riches,
There come now no kings nor Cæsars
Nor gold-giving lords like those gone.
Howe'er in mirth most magnified,
Whoe'er lived in life most lordliest,
Drear all this excellence, delights undurable!
Waneth the watch, but the world holdeth.
Tomb hideth trouble. The blade is laid low.
Earthly glory ageth and seareth.
No man at all going the earth's gait,

The Seafarer

But age fares against him, his face paleth,
Grey-haired he groaneth, knows gone companions,
Lordly men are to earth o'ergiven,
Nor may he then the flesh-cover, whose life ceaseth,
Nor eat the sweet nor feel the sorry,
Nor stir hand nor think in mid heart,
And though he strew the grave with gold,
His born brothers, their buried bodies
Be an unlikely treasure hoard.

From Rihaku

FOUR POEMS OF DEPARTURE

Light rain is on the light dust.
The willows of the inn-yard
Will be going greener and greener,
But you, Sir, had better take wine ere your departure,
For you will have no friends about you
When you come to the gates of Go.

Separation on the River Kiang

Ko-jin goes west from Ko-kaku-ro,
The smoke-flowers are blurred over the river.
His lone sail blots the far sky.
And now 1 see only the river,
       The long Kiang, reaching heaven.

Taking Leave of a Friend

Blue mountains to the north of the walls,
White river winding about them;
Here we must make separation
And go out through a thousand miles of dead grass.

FOUR POEMS OF DEPARTURE

Mind like a floating wide cloud.
Sunset like the parting of old acquaintances
Who bow over their clasped hands at a distance.
Our horses neigh to each other
                    as we are departing.

Leave-taking near Shoku

"Sanso, King of Shoku, built roads"

THEY say the roads of Sanso are steep,
Sheer as the mountains.
The walls rise in a man's face,
Clouds grow out of the hill
                    at his horse's bridle.
Sweet trees are on the paved way of the Shin,
Their trunks burst through the paving,
And freshets are bursting their ice
                    in the midst of Shoku, a proud city.

Men's fates are already set,
There is no need of asking diviners.

FOUR POEMS OF DEPARTURE

The City of Choan

THE phoenix are at play on their terrace.
The phoenix are gone, the river flows on alone.
Flowers and grass
Cover over the dark path
    where lay the dynastic house of the Go.
The bright cloths and bright caps of Shin
Are now the base of old hills.

The Three Mountains fall through the far heaven,
The isle of White Heron
    splits the two streams apart.
Now the high clouds cover the sun
And I can not see Choan afar
And I am sad.

South-Folk in Cold Country

THE Dai horse neighs against the bleak wind of
        Etsu,
The birds of Etsu have no love for En, in the north,
Emotion is born out of habit.
Yesterday we went out of the Wild-Goose gate,
To-day from the Dragon-Pen.[1]
Surprised. Desert turmoil. Sea sun.
Flying snow bewilders the barbarian heaven.
Lice swarm like ants over our accoutrements.
Mind and spirit drive on the feathery banners.
Hard fight gets no reward.
Loyalty is hard to explain.
Who will be sorry for General Rishogu,
                the swift moving,
Whose white head is lost for this province?

`I.e.,` we have been warring from one end of the empire to
the other, now east, now west, on each border.

I HAVE not come to the end of Ernest Fenollosa's notes by a long way, nor is it entirely perplexity that causes me to cease from translation. True, I can find little to add to one line out of a certain poem:

"You know well where it was that I walked
  When you had left me."

In another I find a perfect speech in a literality which will be to many most unacceptable. The couplet is as follows:

"Drawing sword, cut into water, water again flow:
Raise cup, quench sorrow, sorrow again sorry."

There are also other poems, notably the "Five Colour Screen," in which Professor Fenollosa was, as an art critic, especially interested, and Rihaku's sort of Ars Poetica, which might be given with diffidence to an audience of good will. But if I give them, with the necessary breaks for explanation, and a tedium of notes, it is quite certain that the personal hatred in which I am held by many, and the *invidia* which is directed against me because I have dared openly to declare my belief in certain young artists, will be brought to bear first on the flaws of such translation, and will then be merged into depreciation of the whole book of translations. Therefore I give only these unquestionable poems.

E. P.

Sennin Poem by Kakuhaku

THE red and green kingfishers
                flash between the orchids and clover,
One bird casts its gleam on another.

Green vines hang through the high forest,
They weave a whole roof to the mountain,
The lone man sits with shut speech,
He purrs and pats the clear strings.

He throws his heart up through the sky,
He bites through the flower pistil
                and brings up a fine fountain.
The red-pine-tree god looks on him and wonders.
He rides through the purple smoke to visit the
      sennin,
He takes "Floating Hill"* by the sleeve,
He claps his hand on the back of the great water
      sennin.

But you, you dam'd crowd of gnats,
Can you even tell the age of a turtle?

        *Name of a sennin.

A Ballad of the Mulberry Road

(Fenollosa MSS., very early.)

THE sun rises in south east corner of things
To look on the tall house of the Shin
For they have a daughter named Rafu,
      (pretty girl).
She made the name for herself: "Gauze Veil,"
For she feeds mulberries to silkworms,
    She gets them by the south wall of the
      town.

With green strings she makes the warp of her
    basket,
She makes the shoulder-straps of her basket
      from the boughs of Katsura,
And she piles her hair up on the left side of her
    head-piece.

Her earrings are made of pearl,
Her underskirt is of green pattern-silk,
Her overskirt is the same silk dyed in purple,
And when men going by look on Rafu
      They set down their burdens,
They stand and twirl their moustaches.

Old Idea of Choan by Rosoriu

I.

THE narrow streets cut into the wide highway at
   Choan,
Dark oxen, white horses,
      drag on the seven coaches with outriders.
The coaches are perfumed wood,
The jewelled chair is held up at the crossway,
Before the royal lodge
      a glitter of golden saddles, awaiting the
        princess,
They eddy before the gate of the barons.
The canopy embroidered with dragons
     drinks in and casts back the sun.

Evening comes.
     The trappings are bordered with mist.
The hundred cords of mist are spread through
     and double the trees,
Night birds, and night women,
     spread out their sounds through the
     gardens.

Old Idea of Choan by Rosoriu

Birds with flowery wing, hovering butterflies
      crowd over the thousand gates,
Trees that glitter like jade,
      terraces tinged with silver,
The seed of a myriad hues,
A net-work of arbours and passages and covered
   ways,
Double towers, winged roofs,
      border the net-work of ways:
A place of felicitous meeting.
Riu's house stands out on the sky,
      with glitter of colour
As Butei of Kan had made the high golden lotus
      to gather his dews,
Before it another house which I do not know:
How shall we know all the friends
      whom we meet on strange roadways?

To-Em-Mei's "The Unmoving Cloud"

"Wet springtime," says To-em-mei,
        "Wet spring in the garden."

I.

THE clouds have gathered, and gathered,
        and the rain falls and falls,
The eight ply of the heavens
        are all folded into one darkness,
And the wide, flat road stretches out.
I stop in my room toward the East, quiet, quiet,
I pat my new cask of wine.
My friends are estranged, or far distant,
I bow my head and stand still.

II.

Rain, rain, and the clouds have gathered,
The eight ply of the heavens are darkness,
The flat land is turned into river.
        "Wine, wine, here is wine!"
I drink by my eastern window.
I think of talking and man,
And no boat, no carriage, approaches.

To-Em-Mei's "The Unmoving Cloud"

III

The trees in my east-looking garden
               are bursting out with new twigs,
They try to stir new affection,

And men say the sun and moon keep on moving
               because they can't find a soft seat.

The birds flutter to rest in my tree,
               and I think I have heard them saying,
"It is not that there are no other men
But we like this fellow the best,
But however we long to speak
He can not know of our sorrow."

                              T'ao Yuan Ming.
                              A. D. 365– 427.

Transcripts of Fenollosa's Notes

NOTES FOR "SONG OF THE BOWMEN OF SHU"

(chou)

"Shu" dynasty arose and Bunno[文王][1] was esteemed as a Saint.

[cǎi wēi cǎi wēi wēi yì zuò zhǐ]

                                so

采　薇　采　薇。薇　亦　作　止*

sai, bi, sai, bi, bi, eki, ~~saku~~ shi,

to pick off, a kind of edible fern, also to grow

We pick off the "Warabi" which first grow from the earth.

*The letter 止 is no meaning, no use, but each phrase being composed of 4 letters, this is put at the
last of phrase.   日　莫　暮

                       sun not

                       bo

[yuē guī yuē guī suì yì mò zhǐ]

曰　歸　曰　歸。歲　亦　莫　止

etsu, ki, etsu, ki, sai, eki, ~~baku~~, shi,

to say, to return,   year, also, come to last.

We say to each other "when will we return to our country?" –

It will be the last of the year.

The rhime is 作 saku and 莫 baku.

[mǐ shì mǐ jiā xiǎn yǔn zhǐ gù]

靡　室　靡　家。玁　狁　之　故

bi, shitsu, bi, ka, ken, in, shi, ko.

without, room, house,   of because

Here we are far from our home because we have the "Ken-in" as our enemy.

室, 家 have figurative sense, i.e. 室 means <u>wife</u> for the part of husband, 家 means <u>husband</u> for the
part of wife. "Ken-in" was a Turkish tribe who lived in the Mongolian desert.

"Kun-iku," "Ken-in," "Kyō-do" are the same tribes, many European scholars approved that the
"Kyō-do" is quite same to "<u>Hun</u>"; but it is very difficult question, some professors are quite opposite.

---

[1] Bunno[文王]: King Wen, the father of the Zhou dynasty. The original of this poem can be
traced to the reign of King Xuan, the eleventh king of the Zhou (ca. 827 B.C.–ca. 782 B.C.).
Its authorship is anonymous.

[bù huáng qǐ jū xiǎn yǔn zhī gù]
不 遑 啓 居。 玁 狁 之 故。
fu, kō, kei, kyo, ken, in, shi, ko
not, to have leisure, to sit down, to stay

We have no leisure to sit down comfortably (as we did at home) because we have Ken-in as our enemy.

N.B.—The guardians go to the boundary of the empire in the last of spring when the "Warabi" grow from the earth. They return to the country in the winter of the next year. It is very disagreeable to be so far from their home during almost two years, but they shall not be angry against the emperor, because the army of "Ken-in" is very formidable and to protect the country against the enemy is their duty.

[cǎi wēi cǎi wēi wēi yì róu zhǐ]
采 薇 采 薇。 薇 亦 柔 止。
sai bi sai bi bi eki jū shi
                          soft

We pick off the "Warabi" which are soft.

[yuē guī yuē guī xīn yì yōu zhǐ]
曰 歸 曰 歸。 心 亦 憂 止。
etsu, ki, etsu, ki, shin, eki, yū, shi
                    mind also sorrow.

When we say the returning our mind is full of sorrow.

[yōu xīn liè liè zài jī zài kě]
憂 心 烈 烈。 載 饑 載 渇
yu, shin, retsu, retsu, sai ki sai katsu
sorrowful mind, strong,   then to be hungry, thirsty

We are very sorrowful, we are hungry and thirsty

[wǒ shù wèi dìng mǐ shǐ guī pìn]
我 戍 未 定。 靡 使 歸 聘
ga ju mi tei bi shi ki hei
our, defense, not yet, finish, not, let, return, to ask.

But our defence is not yet settled, so we cannot let our friends return to our country and ask how our family lives.

[cǎi wēi cǎi wēi wēi yì gāng zhǐ]

采 薇 采 薇。 薇 亦 剛 止

<u>sai</u> <u>bi</u> <u>sai</u> <u>bi</u> <u>bi</u> <u>eki</u> <u>gō</u> <u>shi</u>

                               rough

We pick off the Warabi which have become already rough.

[yuē guī yuē guī suì yì yáng zhǐ]

曰 歸 曰 歸。 歲 亦 陽*2 止

<u>etsu</u> <u>ki</u> <u>etsu</u> <u>ki</u> <u>sai</u> <u>eki</u> <u>yo</u> <u>shi</u>

                         October

We say to each other "when will we return to our country?" –It will be October.

*In "<u>Eki</u>" the Symbol of October is ䷀䷀ i.e. all lines are "In." There is not "yo" at all, but "yo" comes under the earth, therefore October is called contrarily "the month of Yo".

[wáng shì mǐ gǔ bù huáng qǐ chǔ]

王 事 靡 盬。 不 遑 啟 處

<u>wo</u> <u>ji</u> <u>bi</u> <u>ko</u> <u>fu</u> <u>ko</u> <u>kei</u> <u>sho</u>

royal, affair, not, easy, not, to have leisure, sit down, stay.

We must be prudent for our affair (which is the order of our emperor);

we have no leisure to sit down comfortably.

[yōu xīn kǒng jiù wǒ xíng bù lái]

憂 心 孔 疚。 我 行 不 來

<u>yū</u> <u>shin</u> <u>ko</u> <u>kiū</u> <u>ga</u> <u>ko</u> <u>fu</u> <u>lai</u> liu

sorrowful, mind, very, sick, we, go, not, return.

The rhime of this piece is 疚 and 来. The scholars who prefer the new commentary by Shushi (朱子) read 疚 – <u>kyoku</u> and 来 – <u>lyoku</u> to accord rhime; but I think it forced the sound of words. In my short view, it is much better to read 疚 – ki and 来 – li; because lai contract to li, and kiu contract to ki; but I don't know what is the opinion of Prof. Mori.

Our sorrow is very bitter, but we would not return to the country.

[bǐ ěr wéi hé wéi cháng zhī huá]

彼 爾 維* 何。 維 常 之 華。

<u>hi</u> <u>dei</u> <u>wi</u> <u>ka</u> <u>wi</u> <u>jō</u> <u>shi</u> <u>ka</u>.

that, blooming, what, this, a kind of cherry, of, flower.

What is that blooming flower? –That is "niwazakura".

*維 is used for emphasizing the meaning of phrase.

---

2 陽: 10th month in the Chinese lunar year, the last of the seven "yang" months.

[bǐ lù sī hé jūn zǐ zhī chē]
彼 路 斯 何。 君 子 之 車
hi lo shi ka kun-shi shi sha.
that, chariot, is, what, prince, of, carriage.
Whose is that chariot? —that is our generals.

[róng chē jì jià sì mǔ yè yè]
戎 車 既 駕。 四 牡 業 業
jū sha ki ga shi bo gyō gyō.
chariot, already, to tie the horse, four, horse, stout
The horses are tied already to the chariot; they seem to be vigorous.

[qǐ gǎn dìng jū yī yuè sān jié]
豈 敢 定 居。 一 月 三 捷
gai kan tei kyo ichi getsu san shō.
how dare repose one month three victory
Why shall we repose? We must conquer the enemy even three times in a month.

[jià bǐ sì mǔ sì mǔ kuí kuí]
駕 彼 四 牡。 四 牡 睽睽[3]
ga hi shi bo shi bo ki-ki
to tie horse, that, four, horse, four, horse, strong.
That four horses are tied; they are very strong.

[jūn zǐ suǒ yī xiǎo rén suǒ féi]
君 子 所 依。 小 人 所 腓
kun shi sho i shō-jin sho hi
prince that which, ride, subject, depend.
The generals are on their back, and the soldiers are by their side.

[sì mǔ yì yì xiàng mǐ yú fú]
四 牡 翼翼。 象 弭 魚 服。
shi bo yoku-yoku shō ji gyo fuku
four horse skillful ivory edge of arrow, fish
The four horses are well educated; the generals have the ivory arrows and the quivers that are ornamented with the skin of fish.

---

[3] 睽睽: 騤騤.

[qǐ bù rì   jiè   xiǎn yǔn kǒng jí]
豈 不 日   戒。 獫狁   孔 棘。
<u>gai</u> <u>fu</u> <u>jitsu</u> <u>kai</u> <u>ken-in</u>   <u>kō</u> <u>kyoku</u>
how not daily make attention,   very quick.
We must be careful every day, because the enemy is very quick.

[xī   wǒ   wǎng yǐ   yáng liǔ yī yī]
昔   我   往   矣*   楊柳   依依
<u>seki</u> <u>ga</u>   <u>wo</u>   <u>i</u>   <u>yo-liu</u>   <u>i-i</u>
other time,   went   willow   drooping
Other time when we started the willows are drooping by spring wind.
*矣 is no meaning, occupy the place only.

[jīn wǒ lái sī   yǔ xuě   fēi fēi]
今 我 來 思。 雨雪   霏 霏
<u>kon</u> <u>ga</u> <u>lai</u> <u>shi</u> <u>wu- setsu</u> <u>hi</u> <u>hi</u>
now, we, come,   – it snows, much.
But now we come back when it snows.

[xíng dào chí chí zài kě   zài jī]
行 道 遲遲。 載渴   載饑。
<u>kō</u> <u>dō</u> <u>chi-chi</u> <u>sai</u> <u>katsu</u> <u>sai</u> <u>ki</u>
go road slowly then to be thirsty hungry
We go very slowly and we are thirsty and hungry.

[wǒ xīn shāng bēi mò   zhī wǒ āi]
我 心 傷 悲。 莫   知 我 哀。*
<u>ga</u> <u>shin</u> <u>shō</u> <u>hi</u> <u>baku</u> <u>chi</u> <u>ga</u> <u>ai</u>
our, mind, to be sorrowful, not, know, our, grief.
Our mind is full of sorrow, who will know our grief?
*哀 contract to single "i"

[From *Book of Songs* (11th-7th centuries B.C.)]

65

(no name)

[qīng   qīng   hé   pàn   cǎo]
青   青   河   畔   草
sei   sei   ka   han   so
blue   blue   river   bank   grass
                          side

[yù   yù   yuán   zhōng   liǔ]
鬱   鬱   園   中   柳
utsu   utsu   en   chu   riu
luxuriantly   "   garden   in   willow
shady
in willow

[yíng   yíng   lóu   shàng   nǚ]
盈   盈   樓   上   女
yei   yei   ro   jo   jo
fill   "   storied   on   girl
---full---   house
in first bloom
  of youth

[jiǎo   jiǎo   dāng   chuāng   yǒu]
皎   皎   當   窗   牖[4]
ko   ko   to   so   yo
white   "   just   window   door
brilliant   face
luminous

[é   é   hóng   fěn   zhuāng]
娥   娥   紅   粉   妝
ga   ga   ko   fun   sō
beauty   "   red   powder   toilet
of face   (of beni)

---

[4] 牖: Window.

[xiān xiān chū sù shǒu]
纖 纖 出 素 手
sen sen shutsu so shu
slender slender put forth white hand
                   originally
                   meaning
                   "blanch"
                   "grand"
                   or "not dyed"
                   originally white

[xī wéi chāng jiā nǚ]
昔 為 倡 家 女
seki i sho ka jo
In former was courtesan house girl
times (did)

[jīn wéi dàng zi fù]
今 為 蕩 子 婦
kon i to shi fu
now is dissipated son's wife

[dàng zi xíng bù guī]
蕩 子 行 不 歸
to shi ko fu ki
dissipated son go away not return

[kōng chuáng nán dú shǒu]
空 牀 難 獨 守
ku sho nan doku shu
empty bed hard only one keep.
                   alone

[No. 2 of "Nineteen Ancient Poems" (2nd century A.D.)]

NOTES FOR "THE RIVER SONG"

[jiāng   shàng   yín

江　　上　　吟]

<u>Ko</u>   <u>jo</u>   <u>gin</u>   (1) (one number)

(estuary) river above sing (gin : song without music)

<u>"Song at the River"</u>

[mù   lán   zhī   yì   shā   táng   zhōu

木   蘭   之   枻   沙   棠   舟，]

<u>moku</u> <u>ran</u> <u>shi</u> <u>yei</u>   <u>sha</u> <u>to</u>   <u>shu</u>

--magnolia-- no   side of   name of a tree boat

                      a boat   possibly like Keyaki

a (fine) boat of shato wood, with sides of <u>mokuran</u>.

[yù   xiāo   jīn   guǎn   zuò   liǎng   tóu

玉   簫   金   管   坐   兩   頭。]

<u>gioku</u> <u>sho</u>   <u>kin</u> <u>kwan</u> <u>za</u>   <u>rio</u>   <u>to</u>

jewel   flute   gold   pipe   sit   both   heads

                      instrument of   both sides

                      wood

jewelled flute, and gold pipe, and (musicians) sitting in row on both sides,

[měi   jiǔ   zūn   zhōng zhì   qiān   hú

美   酒   尊   中   置   千   斛，]

<u>bi</u>   <u>shu</u>   <u>son</u>   <u>chu</u>   <u>chi</u>   <u>sen</u>   <u>goku</u>

fine   wine   wine tub   in   put   1000   a measure = 100 <u>sho</u>

(and) with fine wine put in casks to amount of 100 <u>sho</u>.

[zài   jì   suí   bō   rèn   qù   liú

載   妓   隨   波   任   去   留。]

<u>sai</u>   <u>gi</u>   <u>zui</u>   <u>ha</u>   <u>nin</u>   <u>kio</u>   <u>riu</u>

carry courtesan follow waves confide oneself go away stop

     singer   to

                          passive let

                          things go

                          laisser-faire

Carrying also singing girls, and following passing course of waves,

-----with--- those that sit,   going or stopping as the boat will.

            on both sides

[xiān rén yǒu dài chéng huáng hè
仙 人 有 待 乘 黄 鶴,]
sen nin yu tai jo ko kaku
Sennin is wait ride yellow stork
Sennin is in need of a yellow stork to ride on

[hǎi kè wú xīn suí bái ōu
海 客 無 心 隨 白 鷗。]
kai kaku mu shin zui haku o
sea guest not mind follow white gull
-fisherman- no
(Whereas) a sea man, without intention, follows the white gulls
contrast   (whether they go or come)

[qū píng cí fù xuán rì yuè
屈 平 詞 賦 懸 日 月,]
Kutsu pei shi fu ken jitsu getsu
Kutsugen prose song hang on sun moon
Kuppei lit: words measured
        rhymed prose
Kutsuen's prose and poems hang together with sun & moon i.e. (are handed down to posterity
never changing in brightness, fame, like sun & moon)

[chǔ wáng tái xiè kōng shān qiū
楚 王 臺 榭 空 山 丘。]
So o dai sha ku san kiu
So province king terrace palace vacantly mountain hill
(whereas) the terraces of palaces of the King of So have left nothing behind but mountains & hills.

[xīng hān luò bǐ yáo wǔ yuè
興 酣 落 筆 搖 五 嶽,]
kio kwan raku hitsu yo go gaku
pleasure at its hight let fall pen make five peaks
merriment   brandished   move
                rapidly
At the height of the merriment, I sweep my pen, and write poems in such powerful strokes as to
cause the 5 peaks to tremble.

[shī chéng xiào ào   líng   cāng   zhōu
詩　成　笑　傲　　凌　滄　洲。]
shi   sei   sho   go   rio   so   shu
poem is made laugh pride   compete blue   a group of islands
               assume proud   with   archipelago
               countenance   prevail
               (a verb)

The poem being now made, I laugh with all pride in my heart, pride which spreads over (as wide as) the blue islands beyond.

[gōng míng fù   guì   ruò   cháng zài
功　名　富　貴　　若　長　在,]
ko   mei   fu   ki   jaku   cho   zai
merit fame   wealth nobility if   long   exist
If merit, fame, wealth, and nobility were to last forever,

[hàn shuǐ   yì   yīng   xī   běi   liú
漢　水　　亦　應　西　北　　流。]
kan   sui   yeki   o   sei   hoku   riu
Kan   water   also   will   west   north   flow
name of the   ought to
Kan ko (Han river)
The water of this Han River ought to flow north west (instead of S. E. as now.)

                     [By Li Bai (701–762)]

               appropriate spring
[shì   cóng   yí   chūn   yuàn
侍　　從　　宜　　春　　苑]
ji   ju   gi   shun   yen,
waiting upon at   Gi   Shun   Garden
               (Emperor)

[fèng zhào   fù
奉　詔　　賦]
ho   sho   bu
following decree compose (poem)
         order

[lóng   chí   liǔ   sè   chū   qīng
龍   池   柳   色   初   青]
riu   chi   riu   shoku   sho   sei
(on the) dragon pond willow color   (for first time) blue
(subject of)

[tīng   xīn   yīng   bǎi   zhuàn   gē
聽   新   鶯   百   囀   歌]
cho   shin   o   hiaku   ten   ka
hear   new nightingale 100   warble,   the song about
         uguisu
         (lark?)

All this is name, or rather description of circumstances of production, instead of a name (with Genso.)

[dōng   fēng   yǐ   lǜ   yíng   zhō   cǎo
東   風   已   綠   瀛   洲   草，]
to   fu   ki   rioku   yei   shu   so (name of supposed Sennin abode)
eastern   wind   already   green   yei   island   grass
The eastern wind has already made green the grass of Yeishu Island.

[zǐ   diàn   hóng   lóu   jué   chūn   hǎo
紫   殿   紅   樓   覺   春   好。]
shi   den   ko   ro   kaku   shun   ko
purple   hall   crimson   storied   feel   spring   balminess
     of palace   house (become)
                             (conscious)
on purple hall, and crimson story one can feel the spring balminess
                 (of aspect)

[chí   nán   liǔ   sè   bàn   qīng   qīng
池   南   柳   色   半   青   青，]
chi   nan   riu   shoku   han   sei   sei
pond   south   willow   color   half   blue   blue
South of the pond (sunny) the willows are already half blue.

[yíng yān niǎo nuó fú qī chéng。]
縈 煙 嫋 娜 拂 綺 城。]
kei yen cho na futsu ki jo
twining smoke tender tenderness of sweep varied fortress
about mist (of female drapery) female body colored imperial
grace cloth abode
personal (beautiful)

Their tender threads entwine about the mist or brush against the
brocade-like palace (on the roof)

[chuí sī bǎi chǐ guà diāo yíng
垂 絲 百 尺 掛 雕 楹,]
sui shi hiaku shaku kei cho yei
hang down threads 100 feet hang on carved balcony rail
hanging in threads of 100 feet (long) they hang on the carved railings of the balconies.
                                    cling

[shàng yǒu hǎo niǎo xiāng hè míng,
上 有 好 鳥 相 和 鳴,]
jo yu ko cho sho wa mei
above there are lovely birds mutually harmonizing sing
Above (these willows) are seen lovely birds singing in mutual harmony.

[jiān guān zǎo dé chūn fēng qíng
間 關 早 得 春 風 情。]
"kwan kwan" so toku shun pu jo
(onomatopoeia for) early acquired spring wind emotion
(singing of birds)
Then "kan kan" already resounds the emotion of the spring winds—
(foretell-) (spring not yet come)(they get the feeling from the wind)

[chūn fēng quǎn rù bì yún qù,]
春 風 卷 入 碧 雲 去,]
shun pu ken niu heki wun kio
spring wind roll go in blue cloud pass away
As the spring wind (carrying in itself these harmonious sounds) blow up into the sky, and pass away.

72

[qiān mén wàn hù   jiē chūn shēng
千　門　萬　戶　　皆　春　聲。]

<u>sem</u>　<u>mon</u>　<u>ban</u>　<u>ko</u>　　<u>kai</u>　<u>shun</u>　<u>sei</u>
1000 gates 10000 doors all　spring voice
(So these sounds are heard) at every one of the gates and doors (of the palaces)
filling them with spring tone

[shì shí   jūn   wáng zài hào   jīng
是　時　君　王　在　鎬　京，]

<u>shi</u>　<u>ji</u>　<u>kun</u>　<u>wo</u>　<u>zai</u>　<u>ko</u>　<u>kei</u>
This time master king is　old name capital
　　　　　　　　　　　　　stops for Choan
　　　　　　　　　　　　　lives
This time the Emperor is in the Ko Capital.

[wǔ yún chuí huī   yào   zǐ   qīng
五　雲　垂　暉　　耀　紫　清。]

<u>go</u>　<u>wun</u>　<u>sui</u>　<u>ki</u>　　<u>yo</u>　<u>shi</u>　<u>sei</u>
five cloud hang brightness shine purple clean
　　　　　　down　　　　against
And the five clouds (sign of peace) hang above and shine against the purple sky.

[zhàng chū   jīn   gōng suí   rì   zhuàn
仗　出　金　宮　隨　日　轉，]

<u>jo</u>　<u>shutsu</u>　<u>kin</u>　<u>kiu</u>　<u>zui</u>　<u>jitsu</u>　<u>ten</u>
imperial going out of gold palace following sun turn
guards
troop
The guards first appear coming out of the golden palace, and their armor's glitters against the sun
(so following) motion

[tiān huí   yù   niǎn rào   huā   xíng
天　回　玉　輦　繞　花　行。]

<u>ten</u>　<u>kwai</u>　<u>gioku</u>　<u>ren</u>　<u>gio</u>　<u>ka</u>　<u>ko</u>
heaven turn jewel sedan going flower proceed
　　　　　　　　chair round
　　　　or hand chariot
　　　　　of Emperor
Heaven (Emperor) courses his jewel (hand drawn) chariot to make
de-tour—going turning about where flowers are.

73

[shǐ   xiàng   péng   lái   kàn   wǔ   hè
始   向   蓬   萊   看   舞   鶴，]
shi   ko   ho   rai   kan   bu   kaku
at first going towards Horai sees dancing stork
                   name given to
                   part of garden
First it (the chariot) proceeds toward Horai, and (the Emperor) sees the dancing stork (flapping wings)

[haí   guò   chǎi   shí   tīng   xīn   yīng
還   過   茝   石   聽   新   鶯。]
kwan   kwa   sai   seki   tei   shin wo
going back pass by name of a rock hear new nightingale
                   in garden   uguisu
Returning he passes by the Sai rock where he for the first time catches the noise of the new nightingale.

[xīn   yīng   fēi   rào   shàng   lín   yuàn
新   鶯   飛   繞   上   林   苑，]
shin   wo   hi   gio   jo   rin   yen
new   nightingale fly going round --jorin-- garden
                              high forest: name of whole garden
This (fresh new spring) nightingales, seeing the Emperor coming, fly about the whole garden (not stay on willows)

[yuàn   rù   xiāo sháo zá   fèng   shēng
願   入   簫   韶   雜   鳳   笙。]
Gwan   niu   sho   sho   zatsu ho   sho
wishing to enter flute tune mixed phoenix flute
                   melody   with bird
As if they wished that their melody might enter into (harmonize with) the flutes tune, and mixed with the mouth organ (12 pipes, form shape of Ho's tail) (The two shos are played together)
Why? because not only is instrument an imperial instrument, but the bird is the King of birds.
                        [By Li Bai (701–762)]

74

[cháng gān xíng
長　干　行]
Chokanko
　　regular 5
　Chokan　name of town　ko: uta:
　　　place　　　narrative song
　long-mt. side

[qiè　　　　fà　　　chū　fù　　　é
妾　　　　髮　　　初　覆　　　額，　]
Sho　　　hatsu　shō　fuku　　gaku
mistress　hair　first　cover　brow
Chinese lady's　I or my　beginning
My hair was at first covering my brows.
　(child's method of wearing hair)

[zhé　　huā　　mén　　qián　　jù
折　　花　　門　　前　　劇。]
Setsu　kwa　　mon　　zen　　geki
break　flowers　gate　front　play
Breaking flower branches I was frolicking in front of our gate.

[láng　　　qí　　zhú　　mǎ　　lái
郎　　　騎　　竹　　馬 5　來，　]
rō　　　　ki　　chiku　ba　　rai
second person　ride on　bamboo　horse　come
masculine
you young man
lit. young man
When you came riding on bamboo stilts

5　竹馬：A bamboo stick as a toy horse.

75

[rào   chuáng   nòng   qīng   méi

遶   牀[6]   弄   青   梅。]

<u>Gio</u>   <u>sho</u>   ro   <u>sei</u>   <u>bai</u>

going round seat   play with   blue   plums (fruit)

And going about my seat, you played with the blue plums.

[tóng   jū   cháng   gān   lǐ

同   居   長   干   里，]

<u>Do</u>   kiô   <u>cho</u>   <u>kan</u>   <u>ri</u>

same   dwell   cho   kan   village

Together we dwelt in the same Chokan village.

[liǎng   xiǎo   wú   xián   cāi

兩   小   無   嫌   猜。]

rio   <u>sho</u>   <u>mu</u>   <u>ken</u>   <u>sai</u>

double   small   not   dislike   suspicion

"the two"

And we two little ones had neither mutual dislike or suspicion.

(no evil thots or bashfulness)

[shí   sì   wéi   jūn   fù

十   四   為   君   婦，]

ju   <u>shi</u>   i   <u>kun</u>   <u>fu</u>

fourteen   became   lord's   wife

                            your

At fourteen I became your wife.

[xiū   yán   wèi   cháng   kāi

羞   顏   未   嘗   開。]

<u>shu</u>   <u>gan</u>   <u>mi</u>   <u>jo</u>   <u>kai</u>

bashful   face   not yet   ever   open

Bashful I never opened my face (I never laughed)

---

[6] 牀: A household well's railings.

[dī   tóu   xiàng   àn   bì
低   頭   向   暗   壁，]
<u>Tei</u>   to   <u>ko</u>   am   <u>peki</u>
lowering head   face   blank   wall
but lowering my head I always faced toward a dark wall ashamed to see anybody—she sat in
dark corners

[qiān   huàn   bù   yī   huí
千   喚   不   一   迴。]
<u>Sen</u>   <u>kan</u>   <u>fu</u>   itsu   <u>kai</u>
thousand   call   not   once   look back
And though a thousand times called, not once did I look around.

[shí   wǔ   shǐ   zhǎn   méi
十   五   始   展   眉，]
ju   <u>go</u>   <u>shi</u>   tem   <u>bi</u>
    15   first time   open   eyebrows
At fifteen I first opened my brows
i.e. I first knew what married life meant -- now she opens her eyebrows. i.e. smoothes out the
wrinkles between her brows. She now began to understand love, and to be happy.

[yuàn   tóng   chén   yǔ   huī
願   同   塵   與   灰。]
<u>Gan</u>   <u>do</u>   jin   <u>yō</u>   <u>bai</u>
desire   same   dust   together with   ashes
                        and
And so I desired to live and die with you even after death, I wish to be with you even as dust, and
even as ashes—partially together.

[cháng   cún   bào   zhù   xìn
常   存   抱   柱   信，[7]
<u>Jo</u>   son   ho   <u>chu</u>   <u>shin</u>
eternally preserve embrace   pillar   faith
I always had in me the faith of holding to pillars.

_____

7   抱柱信： Faith in your faithfulness. The reference is to a man called Weisheng, who allowed
himself to be drowned in rising floods holding onto a pillar under a bridge waiting for his lover.

77

[qǐ   shàng   wàng   fū   tái
豈   上   望   夫   臺。]
<u>Ki</u>   <u>jo</u>   <u>bo</u>   <u>fu</u>   <u>dai</u>
why should climb lookout husband terrace
And why should I think of climbing the husband looking out terrace.

[shí   liù   jūn   yuǎn   xíng
十   六   君   遠   行，]
<u>ju</u>   <u>roku</u>   <u>kun</u>   <u>en</u>   <u>ko</u>
   16   you   far   go.
At 16, however, you had to go far away.

fearful riverside both yen & yo are adj. expressing form of water
                                         passing over hidden rocks
[qū   táng   yàn   yù   duī
瞿   塘   灩   澦   堆。]
<u>ku</u>   <u>to</u>   <u>yen</u>   <u>yo</u>   <u>tai</u>
 --name--   yenyo-rock
of locality   eddy?
(towards Shoku passing through the difficult place of Yenyotai at Kuto.)

[wǔ   yuè   bù   kě   chù
五   月[8]   不   可   觸，]
<u>go</u>   <u>getsu</u>   <u>fu</u>   <u>ka</u>   <u>shoku</u>
5   month   not   must   touch
In May not to be touched.
The ship must be careful of them in May.

[yuán   shēng   tiān   shàng   āi
猨[9]   聲   天   上   哀。]
<u>en</u>   <u>sei</u>   <u>ten</u>   <u>jo</u>   <u>ai</u>
monkeys voices heaven above sorrowful
Monkeys cry sorrowful above heaven.

---

[8] 五月：Fifth month in the Chinese lunar year.
[9] 猨：Monkeys on the mountainous banks up the river where you are.

[mén   qián   chí   xíng   jì
門   前   遲   行   跡,]
mon   zen   chi   ko   seki
gate   front   late   go   footstep
               reluctant

Your footsteps, made by your reluctant departure, in front of our gate.

[yī   yī   shēng   lǜ   tái
一   一   生   綠   苔。]
itsu   itsu   sei   rioku   tai
one   one   grow   green   mosses

one by one have been grown up into green moss.

[tái   shēn   bù   néng   sǎo
苔   深   不   能   掃,]
Tai   shin   fu   no   so
mosses   deep   not   can   wipe away

These mosses have grown so deep that it is difficult to wipe them away.

[luò   yè   qiū   fēng   zǎo
落   葉   秋   風   早。]
Raku   yo   shu   fu   so
Fallen   leaves   autumn   wind   early

And the fallen leaves indicate autumn wind which (to my thought only) appears to come earlier than usual.

[bā   yuè   hú   dié   huáng
八   月   胡   蝶   黃,]
hachi   gatsu   ko   cho   ko
8th   month   butterflies   yellow

It being already August, the butterflies are yellow

[shuāng   fēi   xī   yuán   cǎo
雙   飛   西   園   草。]
so   hi   sei   yen   so
pairs   fly   western   garden   grass

And yellow as they are, they fly in pairs on the western garden grass.

[gǎn   cǐ   shāng   qiè   xīn
感   此   傷   妾   心,]
kan   shi   sho   sho   shin
affected (by) this hurt (female) mind
                   pained   my
affected at this (absence) my heart pains.

[zuò   chóu   hóng   yán   lǎo
坐   愁   紅   顏   老。]
za   shu   ko   gan   ro
gradually lament crimson face decay—older
                          become old.
The longer the absence lasts, the deeper I mourn, my early fine pink face,
will pass to oldness, to my regret.

[zǎo   wǎn   xià   sān   bā
早   晚   下   三   巴,]
so   ban   ka   sam   pa
sooner (or) later descend three whirls
                       name of spot on Yangtse Kiang, where waters whirl
If you be coming down as far as the Three Narrows sooner or later,

[yù   jiāng   shū   bào   jiā
預   將   書   報   家。]
yo   sho   shō   ho   ka
beforehand with letter report family-home
Please let me know by writing

[xiāng yíng   bù   dào   yuǎn
相   迎   不   道   遠,]
sho   gei   fu   do   yen
mutually meeting not say far
         coming to meet

For I will go out to meet, not saying that the way be far.

caring

[zhí   zhì   cháng fēng shā
直   至   長   風   沙。]
<u>choka</u>   <u>chi</u>   <u>cho</u>   <u>fu</u>   <u>sa</u>
directly arrive long wind sand

--a port on the Yangtse--

And will directly come to Chofusha.

(the port just this side of Sampa)

[By Li Bai (701–762)]

[yù   jiē   yuàn

玉   階   怨]

gioku   kai   yen

Jewel stairs grievance

        ladder grief, slightly tinged with hatred, resent

[yù   jiē   shēng   bái   lù

玉[10]   階   生   白   露，]

gioku   kai   sei   haku   ro

jewel steps grow white dew

The jewel stairs have already become white with dew.

        (dew was thought to grow on things)

[yè   jiŭ   qīn   luó   wà

夜   久   侵   羅   襪。]

ya   kiu   shin   ra   betsu

night long permeate transparent stocking.

        attack   gauze

Far gone in the night, the dew has come up to my gauze sock.

[què   xià   shuĭ   jīng   lián

卻   下   水   晶   簾，]

kiaku   ka   sui   sho   ren

let   down water crystal sudare

         --crystal--

So I let down the crystal curtain

[líng   lóng wàng   qiū   yuè

玲   瓏   望   秋   月。]

rei   ro   bo   shu   getsu

transparent clear look at autumn   moon

And still look on the bright moon shining beyond.

           [Li Bai (701–762)]

---

[10] 玉: White marble.

<u>Gioku</u> <u>kai</u> means here a place where court ladies are living, one of the imperial mistresses. The subject of the poem is that one of them was waiting in vain for the lord to come. The beauty of the poem lies in not a single character being used to explain the idea of waiting and resenting; yet the poem is full of the idea. This is how. Thinking that the lord will come, she was coming out to meet him at the entrance, a flight of steps ornamented with gems. She was standing there till the very dewiness of night wets her stockings. She lets down her curtain already despairing of his coming. And yet she can see the moon shining so bright outside, and had to think of the possibility of the lord's still coming, because it is so fine a night; and so passes the whole night awake.

[gǔ   fēng   zhī   shí bā

古　　风　　之　　18]

18th Kofu

[tiān   jīn   sān   yuè   shí

天　　津　　三　　月　　時，]

ten   shin   san   getsu   ji

name of bridge in   3rd   month   time

  Rakuyo   March

"Heaven ferry"

At Tenshin bridge in March time

[qiān   mén   táo   yǔ   lǐ

千　　門　　桃　　與　　李。]

sen   mon   to   yō   ri

1000   gates   peaches with   apricots

The 1000 gates have peaches & apricots

  (gates of mansions)

[zhāo   wéi   duàn   cháng   huā

朝　　為　　斷　　腸　　花，]

cho   i   dan   cho   ka

morning become   cut   intestine   flowers

                 rend

                        intense emotion

In the morning they are unbearably beautiful flowers

mù   zhú   dōng   liú   shuǐ

暮　　逐　　東　　流　　水。]

bō   chiku   to   riu   sui

evening pursue   east   flowing   water

         drive on

But by evening they decay and follow the eastern flowing water

[qián shuǐ   fù   hòu   shuǐ

前　水　　復　　後　　水，]

zen   sui   fuku   ko   sui

front water   also   behind   water
The front going water and hind going water
water in continual flow, mass after mass,

[gǔ   jīn   xiāng   xù   liú
古   今   相   續   流。]
ko   kon   sho   zoku   riu
old   new   mutually   connecting flow
water past and present in continuous flow.

[xīn   rén   fēi   jiù   rén]
新   人   非   舊   人，]
shin   jin   hi   kiu   jin
new   man   are not   past   man
The men of today are not the men of the past

[nián   nián   qiáo   shàng   yóu
年   年   橋   上   遊。]
nen   nen   kio   jo   yu
year   year   bridge   on   play
                                  wander
(and yet) year after year, they wander onto same bridge
                  (scene does not change)

[jī   míng   hǎi   sè   dòng
雞   鳴   海   色   動，]
kei   mei   kai   shoku   do
cock   crowing   sea   color   move
  early morning
In early dawn the color of the sky moves

[yè   dì   luó   gōng   hóu
謁   帝   羅   公   侯。]
etsu   tei   ra   ko   ko
wait on emperor   stand   princes   dukes.
                  in row
In order to wait on the emperor princes & earls go about in rank

[yuè   luò   xī   shàng   yáng
月   落   西   上   陽,]
getsu   raku   sei   jo   yo
moon   falls (on)   western   upper   yang

            name of a gate in Rakuyo

The moon has fallen behind the western yo man gate

[yú   huī   bàn   chéng   lóu
餘   輝   半   城   樓。]
yo   ki   han   jo   ro
lingering   moonlight   half   city wall   building on top of gate.

And the lingering light is still seen on half of this storied gate.

[yī   guān   zhào   yún   rì
衣   冠   照   雲   日,]
i   kwan   sho   wun   jitsu
dress   hat   shine   cloud   sun

            against

(by and by they return) with the dresses & head coverings glittering against cloud and sun

[cháo   xià   sàn   huáng   zhōu
朝   下   散   皇   州。]
cho   ka   san   ko   shu
court   descending   disperse   imperial   province

            --capital--

descending from court they disperse themselves throughout the capital.

[ān   mǎ   rú   fēi   lóng
鞍   馬   如   飛   龍,]
am   ba   jō   hi   rio
harnessed horse   like   flying   dragon

The horses they ride on, are like flying dragons.

[huáng jīn   luò   mǎ   tóu
黄   金   絡   馬   頭。]
o   gon   raku   ba   to
yellow metal   tied to   horse   head

gold trappings are tied to the horses' heads.

[xíng rén jiē bì yì
行 人 皆 辟 易,]
ko jin kai heki eki
going men all go aside change
             --stand aside--
The street men all stand aside (in amazement)

[zhì qì héng sōng qiū
志 氣 横 嵩 丘。]
shi ki o su kiu
will mental lie high hill.
    state parallel name
    aspect to
Their mental air is lofty as yonder Su hill (near Rakuyo)

[rù mén shàng gāo táng
入 門 上 高 堂,]
niu mon jo ko do
entering gate ascend high hall
Entering the honor gates they go up into high hall

[liè dǐng cuò zhēn xiū
列 鼎 錯 珍 羞。]
retsu tei saku chin shu
In row urns (contain) curious food
          mixed excellent
There the rows of urns have mixed rare dainties.

[xiāng fēng yǐn zhào wǔ
香 風 引 趙 舞,]
ko fu in cho bu
fragrant wind draw cho (girls) dance
(While feasting goes on songs are sung & flutes are played)
As the girls from Cho dance the fragrant wind draws

[qīng guǎn suí qí ōu
清 管 隨 齊 謳。]
sei kwan zui sei o
clear flute follow sei (girls) song
As the Sei girls sing, the clear flute follows.

87

[qī　　shí　　zǐ　　yuān　　yāng

七　　十　　紫　　鴛　　鴦,]

shichi　ji　　shi　　yen　　wo

seven　-ty　purple　male　female
　　　　　　　　　　duck　duck

Seventy purple mandarin ducks

[shuāng　shuāng　xì　　tíng　　yōu

雙　　　雙　　　戲　　庭　　幽。]

so　　so　　gi　　tei　　yu

double double frolic garden corners

In pairs & pairs they frolic in corners of the gardens

(probably implies that men and women go off in pairs)

xíng　　lè　　zhēng　　zhòu　　yè

行　　樂　　爭　　畫　　夜,]

ko　　raku　　so　　chu　　ya

exercising pleasure struggle day night

practising　　　　force

In practise of pleasures they force night into day.

[zì　yán　　dù　　　qiān　qiū

自　言　度　　千　秋。]

ji　　gen　　do　　sen　　shu

self　say　pass over 1000 autumns

They themselves say that they will thus pass through the 1000 autumns.

[gōng　chéng　　shēng　bù　tuì

功　　成　　　身　不　退,]

ko　　sei　　shin　　fu　　tai

merit accomplished body　not　retiring.

deed　　　　　　self

The deed accomplished and the body isnt retiring

[zì　　gǔ　　duō　qiān　yóu

自　古　多　怨　尤。]

ji　　ko　　ta　　yen　　yu

from old time many errors failures

If so, such life was from oldest days known to be full of errors & failures.

[huáng quǎn kōng tàn xī
黄 犬 空 歎 息,]
ko ken ku tan soku
yellow dogs vacant sigh in spiritus
----lament----
The yellow dog to no purport, lamenting.
(Refers to life of Rishi [Li Si] a favorite of Shikotei [First Emperor of China] but did not retire
with death of Emperor.)

[lǜ zhū chéng xìn chóu
綠 珠 成 釁 讐。]
rioku shu sei kin shu
green jewel become disgracious enemy
-female name- produce animosity
Riokushu became the cause of disgrace and hatred
(Here another reference to S. [Shi Chong], a very rich statesman in time of Sateo Shin, who had
a very beautiful concubine, called Riokushu, but one of the princes of his master intended to have
her and, on S. refusing, the prince charged him with false crime, and destroyed him. This said that
the mistress on seeing the soldiers coming, threw herself down and killed herself.)

[hé rú chī yí zǐ
何 如 鴟 夷 子,]
ka jo shi i shi.
How (is it) Hanrei bottle Mr.
name of a philosopher Hanrei
phil. of the wine bottle
How are such things (those men and dog) compared with what Shi i shi
has done.

[sàn fà zhào piān zhōu
散 髮 櫂 扁 舟。]
sam patsu to hen shu
untied hair pole flat boat.
Who with untrimmed hair poled away his flat boat?
(Hanrei [Fan Li] was rich, and after accomplishing his deed, went away rowing no one knows
where, with his mistress)

[Li Bai (701–762)]

[gǔ   fēng   zhī   shí sì

古　　风　　之　　14]

14th Kofu

[hú   guān   ráo   fēng   shā

胡　　關　　饒　　風　　沙，]

kō   kwan   gio   fu   shā

north   gate   much   wind   sand

barbarian

regions around

"Fort gate against barbarians abound in wind and sand".

[xiāo   suǒ   jìng   zhōng   gǔ

蕭　　索　　竟　　終　　古。]

sho   saku   kio   shu   kō

serene -----   finally   end   old

lonely   till now

"Lonely from the beginning of time till now"

[mù   luò   qiū   cǎo   huáng

木　　落[11]　　秋　　草　　黄，]

moku   raku   shu   so   kō

tree   fall   autumn   grass   yellow

"The trees fall, and autumn grasses are yellow"

       drop leaves

[dēng   gāo   wàng   róng   lǔ

登　　高　　望　　戎　　虜。]

to   kō   bo   ju   riō

ascend   high   lookout   barbarous   prisoner

                --enemies' force--

"Ascending on high, & looking out toward where the barbarians lived"

---

[11] 木落：Trees stripped of leaves.

[huāng chéng kōng dà   mò
荒   城   空   大   漠,]
ko   jo   ku   tai   baku
desolate castle sky   large desert
                 vacant
"I see a ruined fortress in a vast blank desert"

[biān   yì   wú   yí   dǔ
邊   邑   無   遺   堵。]
hen   yu   mū   i   tō
frontier village not   left wall
"The frontier villages have not even walls left"

[bái   gǔ   héng qiān shuāng
白   骨   橫   千   霜,]
haku   kotsu o   sen   so
white   bones lie   thousand frost (years)
"The white bones lie there through a thousand frosts"

[cuó   é   bì   zhēn mǎng
嵯   峨   蔽   榛   莽。]
sa   ga   hei   shun bo
steep   steep cover trees grass
(bones) "making steep heaps, covered by thorny trees and grass."

[jiè   wèn   shuí líng nüè
借   問   誰   凌   虐,]
sa   mon   sui   rio   giaku
suppose ask   who   ---devastate---
"Let me ask who has caused this cruel devastation? (speaking to himself)

[tiān   jiāo dú   wēi   wǔ
天   驕   毒   威   武。]
ten   kio   doku i   bu
heaven active poisonous power military
        horse   influence force
-barbarian kings-
It is the barbarian kings spreading the poisonous influence of their
military power.
Poet here apologizes in words, but condemns in intent.

[hè nù wǒ shèng huáng
赫 怒 我 聖 皇,]
kaku dō ga sei kō
burning anger our sacred Emperor
So as to have caused our sage Emperor to burn with anger. (appears to praise Emp.)

[láo shī shì pí gǔ
勞 師 事 鼙 鼓。]
ro shi ji hei ko
giving work to army make drum different kind of drum
letting serve business of
Resulting in his employment of forces in devotion to warfare.

[yáng hé biàn shā qì
陽 和 變 殺 氣,]
yo wa hen satsu ki
yang mild change slaughtering atmosphere
-----spring---- into ----autumn-----
The balmy spring changes suddenly into slaughtering autumn
                                                    bloodthirsty

[fā zú sāo zhōng tǔ
發 卒 騷 中 土。]
hatsu sotsu so chu do
send out soldiers disturb middle realm
Sending out soldiers, thereby causing disturbance in the middle realm.

[sān shí liù wàn rén
三 十 六 萬 人,]
san ju roku wan nin
360,000 men
Those 360,000 men. no verb—only suggestion

[āi āi lèi rú yǔ
哀 哀 淚 如 雨。]
ai ai rui jo u
melancholy melancholy tears like rain
One is filled with sorrow, and tears run down like rain

[qiě bēi jiù xíng yì
且 悲 就 行 役,]
sa hi ju ko eki
end regret follow go service
(light meaning)   ---conscription---
At both ends -- the going out for service and the consequent lack of hands for
agriculture-- make one regret.

[ān dé yíng nóng pǔ
安 得 營 農 圃。]
an toku yei no ho
how can occupy farm yard
with

[bù jiàn zhēng shù ér
不 見 征 戍 兒,]
fu ken sei ju ji
not see offensive defensive child
------soldiers------
Without seeing the soldiers personally

[qǐ zhī guān shān kǔ
豈 知 關 山 苦。]
ki chi kwan zan ku
how know fortress gate mountain hardship
How can one know the hardship of the fortress mt.?
    (Emperor at palace can't know)

[lǐ mù jīn bù zài
李 牧 今 不 在,]
Ri- boku kin fu zai
---name--- now not exist
(Riboku [Li Mu] is name of a general who was sent out in old centuries against barbarians,
and who, instead of trying to use armed forces, knew how to pacify them.)

93

[biān rén   sì   chái   hǔ
邊   人   飼   豺   虎。]
<u>hen</u> <u>jin</u>   <u>shi</u>   <u>sai</u>   <u>ko</u>
frontier men make food of wolves tigers
         nourish

This is like giving frontier guards as food for wolves and tigers (i.e. barbarians.)

[Li Bai (701–762)]

94

[yì   jiù   yóu   jì   qiáo   jùn   yuán   cān   jūn
憶   舊   遊   寄   譙   郡   元   參   軍]
oku   kiu   yu   ki   sho   gun   gen   san   gun
recollecting past travel write name district family council bar
       old pleasure- to   name --title—
            making
Remembering former play write to chancellor Gen of Sho district
                        (epistle)

[yì   xì   luò   yáng   dǒng   zāo qiū
憶   昔   洛   陽   董   糟 丘,]
oku   seki   raku   yo   to   so kiu
recollect ancient Rakuyo   name   lit. name
                          of family husk-hill
                                   what remains after wine is extracted
I now remember that it was To-so Kiu of Rakuyo

[wèi yú tiān   jīn   qiáo   nán   zào   jiŭ   lóu
爲   餘   天   津   橋   南   造   酒   樓。]
I   yō   ten   shin   kio   nan   zo   shu   ro
For me heaven port   bridge south make   wine   storied
                                      build   house
(Who) for me specially built a tavern to the South of the Tenshin bridge.

[huáng jīn   bái   bì   mǎi   gē   xiào
黄   金   白   璧   買   歌   笑,]
o   gon   haku   heki   bai   ka   sho
yellow gold   white jewel buy   songs laughter
(Where) buying song and laughter with gold and jewels

[yī   zùi   lěi   yuè   qīng   wáng   hóu
一   醉   累   月   輕   王   侯。
itsu sui   rui   getsu   kei   o   ko
one drink successive months disdain kings (&) princes.
once drunk
(And) once drunk for months together I despised Kings & princes

[hǎi nèi xián háo qīng yún kè
海 內 賢 豪 青 雲 客,]
kai nai ken go sei wun kaku
sea interior wise great blue cloud guest
From all parts of the Empire came flocking wise and great guests in prosperous court life (to me
while I was there)

[jiù zhōng yǔ jūn xīn mò nì
就 中 與 君 心 莫 逆。]
shu chu yo kun shin baku giaku
take middle with lord mind not run counter
"especially" you oppose
And amongst them it was with you especially that our minds had nothing running counter.

[húi shān zhuǎn hǎi bù zuò nán
迴 山 轉 海 不 作 難,]
kwai zan ten kai fu saku nan
to make mt. to make sea not make hard
roll turn consider
(You) considering it nothing even if you had to roll over mts and turn back the oceans for me,
(determined to go through hardships for my sake)

[qīng qíng dào yì wú suǒ xī
傾 情 倒 意 無 所 惜。]
kei jo to i mu sho saku
entering emotion invest mind not what lament
"make incline" give entirely will regret
pour into: here to
"tip"
And pour out all your emotion & will, without regret (devote your mind for me)

[wǒ xiàng huái nán pān guì zhī
我 向 淮 南 攀 桂 枝,]
ga ko wai nan hon kei shi
I facing name of south climb katsura leaves
river up laurel
I facing the region south of the Wai, climbed the laurel trees (they are abundant there and there is
a poem of same emotion by old king of Wainan) and a poetical way of saying he had to go there.

96

[jūn   liú   luò   běi   chóu   mèng sī
君   留   洛   北   愁   夢 思。]
kun <u>riu</u>   <u>raku</u>   <u>hoku</u> <u>shu</u>   <u>mu</u> <u>shi</u>
lord   remaining name of north feeling sorry dream thought
you   water

And you remained North of the Raku now, so that we had to undergo of thinking of each other in dream(ing)

[bù   rěn   bié
不   忍   別,
<u>fu</u>   <u>jin</u>   <u>betsu</u>
not   forbear separate

And as we could not forbear being separated

[hái   xiāng   suí
還   相   隨。
<u>kan</u> <u>sho</u>   <u>zui</u>
again mutually follow

We again came together.

[xiāng suí   tiáo   tiáo fǎng xiān   chéng
相   隨   逈   逈   訪 仙   城,]
<u>sho</u>   <u>zui</u>   <u>sho</u>   <u>sho</u> <u>ho</u>   <u>sen</u>   <u>jo</u>
mutually following far-far   visit sennin fortress
               very   name of mt.

And accompanying each other we travelled far into the Sennin Mts.

[sān shí liù   qǔ   shuǐ húi   yíng
三   十   六   曲   水   迴   縈。]
<u>san</u> <u>ju</u>   <u>roku</u> <u>kioku</u> <u>sui</u> <u>kwai</u> <u>yei</u>
36   (fold) bent   water twining bent toward

Where the 36 fold bending waters twine & twist.

[yī   xī   chū rù   qiān huā   míng
一   溪   初   入   千   花   明,]
<u>itsu</u> <u>kei</u> <u>sho</u> <u>niu</u> <u>sen</u> <u>ka</u>   <u>mei</u>
one   valley first entered 1000 flowers bright
  (watery valley)

On entering the first valley (one already sees the scene to be entirely changed) there being 1000 different bright flowers.

97

[wàn   hè   dù   jìn   sōng   fēng   shēng
萬   壑   度   盡   松   風   聲。]
ban   goku   do   jin   sho   fu   sei
10000 valleys   pass   lit.: "spent" pine   wind   voice
  (rocky valleys) through entirely

And after passing through innumerable rocky valleys one comes to a calm region where one hears nothing but the voice of the pine winds.

[yín   ān   jīn   luò   dǎo   píng   dì
銀   鞍   金   絡   倒   平   地,]
gin   an   kin   raku   to   hei   chi
silver harness gold   reins   bow   flat   ground
        saddle   prostrate
                              lit.: "inverted"
                              "upside down"

(Presently) comes the governor of the East of the Kan To

[hàn   dōng   tài   shǒu   lái   xiāng   yíng
漢   東   太   守   來   相   迎。]
kan   to   tai   shu   rai   sho   gei
Han River East grand   guard   come   mutually meet
                governor

Meet us riding (on horses) of silver saddle & gold rein, and prostrating himself on the flat ground.

[zǐ   yáng   zhī   zhēn   rén
紫   陽   之   真   人,]
shi   yo   shi   shin   jin
Purple yang's   true   man
name of mt.   --sennin--

There also came the Sennin of Shiyo to meet me

[yāo   wǒ   chuī   yù   shēng
邀   我   吹   玉   笙。]
Yo   ga   sui   gioku   sho
coming me   play   jewel   mouth organ
to meet

Playing on a jewelled mouth organ

98

[cān xiá lóu shàng dòng xiān yuè
餐 霞 樓 上 動 仙 樂，]

san ka ro jo do sen gaku
feast mist storied on move sennin music
--name-- house

In Sanka storied house they gave us entertainment of sennin music

[cáo rán wǎn shì luán fèng míng
嘈 然 宛 似 鸞 鳳 鳴。]

so gen en ji ram fo mei
loud symphonic adj. exactly resemble young ho singing
sounds of ending phoenix crying
many notes like

Whose loud symphony resembled the crying of young & old ho birds (phoenix) singing

[xiù cháng guǎn cuī yù qīng jǔ
袖 長 管 催 欲 輕 舉，]

shu cho kwan sai yoku kei kiō
sleeves long (by)pipe becoming wont to light(ly) rise
tribe of excited about to
the sho

The governor of Kanchu, drunk, stands and

[hàn zhōng tài shǒu zuì qǐ wǔ
漢 中 太 守12 醉 起 舞。]

kan chu tai shu sui kī bu
Kan middle great defender drunk stand dance
province guard up

dances, because his long sleeves, excited by the pipes, could not but rise lightly of its own accord

[shǒu chí jǐn páo fù wǒ shēn
手 持 錦 袍 覆 我 身，]

shu ji kim po fuku ga shin
hand holding brocade upper cover my body
garment self

I, drunk, lay down, with my head pillowed on his thigh

---

12 太守: Governor.

[wǒ zuì héng   mián   zhěn   qí   gǔ
我 醉 横   眠   枕   其   股。]
ga   sui   o   min   chin   ki   ko
I   drunk horizontal sleep   pillow   its   thigh
        laying down   (rest)   his
And he with his brocade garment in hand covered me.

[dāng   yán   yì   qì   líng   jiǔ   xiāo
當   筵   意   氣   凌   九   霄,]
to   yen   i   ki   rio   kiu   sho
this day lit "carpet" will spirit   prevail   9   sky
occasion dinner   state of mind
          entertainment
At this entertainment I felt as if my spiritedness permeated all through the 9 heavens

[xīng   lí   yǔ   sàn   bù   zhōng zhāo
星   離   雨   散   不   終   朝,]
sei   ri   u   san   fu   shu   cho
stars separate rain disperse not   end   morning-day
(but) before the end of the day (before evening) we had to disperse like stars and rain.

[fēn   fēi   chǔ   guān   shān   shǔi   yáo
分   飛   楚   關   山   水   遙。]
bun   pi   sō   kan   san   sui   yo
separate fly   name of place   mt   water   far off
        So's fortress gate
I had to fly apart toward the So frontier, and mts. & waters put us far apart.

[yú   jì   huán   shān   xún   gù   cháo
餘   既   還   山   尋   故   巢,]
yo   ki   kwan   zan   jin   ko   so
I   already return   mt.   ask after   old   nest
                   search
I already returned to the mt and had to search for my old nest.

[jūn	yì	gūi	jiā	dù	wèi	qiáo
君	亦	歸	家	渡	渭	橋。]
kun	yeki	ki	ka	do	I	kio
lord	also	return	home	pass over	name	bridge
you					of river	

And you, going home, would have passed over the I bridge.

2ᴺᴰ PART OF POEM

[jūn	jiā	yán	jūn	yǒng	pí	hǔ
君	家	嚴	君	勇	貔	虎，]
kun	ka	gen	kun	yu	hi	kō
lord's	house	strict-lord		brave	leopard	tiger
your		your father				

Your father "brave like leopards and tigers" (used in Shoku classic of generals)

[zuò	yǐn	bìng	zhōu	è	róng	lǔ
作	尹	並	州	遏	戎	虜。]
saku	in	hei	shu	kwatsu	fu	riō
having	governor	name of	province	put down	barbarians	prisoners
become		province				hordes

Having become the governor of Heishu, was occupied in putting down the barbarian hordes.

[wǔ	yuè	xiāng	hū	dù	tài	háng
五	月¹³	相	呼	度	太	行，]
go	getsu	so	kō	tō	tai	ko
five	month	mutually	calling	pass over	great	journey: march

In May he caused you to call me, (travelling) across Taiko (a name of a mt.)

[cuī	lún	bù	dào	yáng	cháng	kǔ
摧	輪	不	道	羊	腸	苦。]
sai	rin	fu	do	yo	cho	kū
break	wheel	not	say	sheep	intestines	difficulty: hardship

Where, although wheels be broken, I will not say the hardship of travelling through mountains
winding like sheep's intestines (sheep's intestines are worst winding)

---

¹³ 五月：5ᵗʰ month.

[xíng lái běi liáng suì yuè shēn
行 來 北 凉 歲 月 深,]
ko rai hoku rio sai getsu shin
go come north cool year month deep
Going (traveling) I come, and where the north wind's already cold, being advanced in year

[gǎn jūn guì yì qīng huáng jīn
感 君 貴 義 輕 黃 金。]
kan kun ki gi kei o gon
feel lord's noble faithful despise yellow gold
      your   to friends disdain
I was struck by your esteem of faithfulness and disdain of gold

[qióng bēi qǐ shí qīng yù àn
瓊 杯 綺 食 青 玉 案,]
ku hai ki shoku sei gioku an
red gems cup beautiful food blue jade stand
jewels   (of clothes)   (enamel)
Red jade cup and fine colored food, placed on blue jewelled table

[shǐ wǒ zuì bǎo wú guī xīn
使 我 醉 飽 無 鳊 心。]
shi ga sui ho mu ki shin
make me drunk full no return mind
have made me drunk and satisfied, and forgetful of returning.

[shí shí chū xiàng chéng xī qū
時 時 出 向 城 西 曲,]
ji ji shutsu ko jo sei kioku
time time go out face castle west corner or meanderings
From time to time you took me out towards western corner of the city

[jìn cí liú shuǐ rú bì yù
晉 祠 流 水 如 碧 玉。]
shin shi riu sui jō heki gioku
dynasty temple flow water is like deep blue jade
Shin   shrine
Where (as I remember) around the Shin Shrine is surrounded by running water, clear as blue gems

[fú   zhōu   nòng   shuǐ   xiāo   gǔ   míng
浮   舟   弄   水   簫   鼓   鳴，]
fu   shu   ro   sui   sho   kō   mei
making boat play water mouth drum sing
float   with   organ   play out, make noise
Then we floated a boat, and played with the water (in hand), sounding our flutes and drums.

[wēi   bō   lóng   lín   suō   cǎo   lǜ
微   波   龍   鱗   莎   草   綠。]
bi   ha   rio   rin   bio   so   rioku
faint waves dragon scales water- grass green
    ripples   floating
The small ripples resembled the scales of dragons, and the water grass was green.

[xīng   lái   xié   jì   zì   jīng   guò
興   來   携   妓   恣   經   過，]
kio   rai   kei   gi   shi   kei   kwa
pleasure come, bring courtezan free of pass pass
      coming with   one's will
At the height of pleasure, we took with us courtezans, and passed along (part of water) in utter
liberty.

[qí   ruò   yáng   huā   shì   xuě   hé
其   若   楊   花   似   雪   何。]
kī   joku   yo   kwa   ji   setsu   ka
That like willow flowers resemble snow how!
How
What shall I do with the willow flowers falling like snow (It's to be regretted that willow flowers
fall—expression of separateness)

[hóng   zhuāng   yù   zuì   yí   xié   rì
紅   粧   欲   醉   宜   斜   日，]
ko   sho   yoku   sui   gi   sha   jitsu
crimson paint want to drink had incline sun
vermillion (on face)   better
The red painted girls about to be drunk, are appropriate to the inclining sun (look beautiful with
glow of sun very fine in color) the red here refers to all 3, all girls red, also drunk, also sun.

[bǎi   chǐ   qīng   tán   xiě   cuì   é

百   尺   清   潭   寫   翠   娥。[14]]

<u>hiaku</u> <u>seki</u> <u>sei</u> <u>tan</u> <u>sha</u> <u>sui</u> <u>ga</u>

hundred feet pure deep copy green eyebrow

               reflect

Where the hundred feet deep clear water are reflected their green eyebrows (the girls.)
(Chinese girls in long form of a brow ...... their eyebrows are shady, and green penciled afterword) eyes of court ladies were done so too.

[cuì   é   chán   juān   chū   yuè   huī

翠   娥   嬋   娟   初   月   輝,]

<u>sui</u> <u>ga</u> <u>sen</u> <u>ken</u> <u>shō</u> <u>getsu</u> <u>ki</u>

green eyebrow beautiful   early moon shine

         (of lady's face)

The green eyebrows are graceful and beautiful, (and like) the new moon shining
(The beauty of the line lies in there being no like—2 assertions, but likeness implied)

[měi   rén   gēng   chàng   wǔ   luó   yī

美   人   更   唱   舞   羅   衣。]

<u>bi</u> <u>jin</u> <u>ko</u>   <u>sho</u> <u>bu</u> <u>ra</u> <u>i</u>

beautiful persons one another sing   dance brocade clothing

   women   transparent

The beauties sing to one another, and some dance with trans. brocade clothes (like no dresses)

[qīng   fēng   chuī   gē   rù   kōng   qù

清   風   吹   歌   入   空   去,]

<u>sei</u> <u>fu</u> <u>sui</u> <u>ka</u> <u>niu</u> ku <u>kiō</u>

pure wind blow poetry enter space go away

          against song   vanish

The clear wind, blowing against the song, rises with it into the sky. (the voice seems to ascend with the wind).

---

[14] 翠娥: Beautiful women.

[gē   qǔ   zì   rào   xíng   yún   fēi
歌   曲   自   繞   行   雲   飛。]
kā   kioku   ji   gio   ko   wun   hī
song melody of itself wind up- going cloud fly
                        involve passing

And the songs and music of themselves fly around the passing cloud. (This is fine line. The one before is made for this) (The cloud itself moves, the music, rising with the air, are heard as if they were whistling twisted in the clouds as it were echoing from clouds)

[cǐ   shí   xíng   lè   nán   zài   yù
此   時   行   樂   難   再   遇,]
shi   ji   ko   raku   nan   sai   gu
this   time pleasure making hard again meet
That time
of that period the pleasures cannot be met again

[xī   yóu   yīn   xiàn   cháng   yáng   fù
西   遊   因   獻   長   楊   賦。]
sei   yu   in   ken   cho   yo   bu
west   travel therefore offer long willow poetry (to be sung)
                                              song

So I travelled westward and offered the Choyo song. (refers to historical fact in late Kan was a scholar called Yoyu who presented on occasion of imperial hunting a fine poem describing scene, the Emperor admiring, admitted him. The poem was called Choyofu—R's poem was not so called, but means any poem for examination)

[běi   què   qīng   yún   bù   kě   qī
北   闕   青   雲   不   可   期,]
hoku   ketsu   sei   wun   fu   ka   ki
north   lit.: gate blue cloud not possible determine
                         promotion   (the time) waited

At the court the promotions could not be expected (was not obtainable as one expected)(he was unsuccessful) (he had employment, but did not get ahead as fast as or in the way he wanted).

[dōng   shān   bái   shǒu   huán   guī   qù
東   山   白   首   還   歸   去。]
to   zan   haku   shū   kwan   ki   kiō
east   mountain white head   return return away
So I had to return to the Eastern mt. with my head already become white.

[wèi qiáo nán tóu yī yù jūn
渭 橋 南 頭 一 遇 君,]
I kio nan to itsu gu kun
I bridge south head once meet you
(On my returning to Loyan) I passed over the I bridge (again) and at the Southern end I once
again met you

[zàn tái zhī běi yòu lí qún
鄭 臺 之 北 又 離 羣。]
san tai shi hoku yu ri gun
San palace 's north again separate from crowd
(But this meeting is not of long duration) because you are to go to the North of the San terrace,
so that (we) the group must separate.

[wèn yú bié hèn zhī duō shǎo
問 餘 別 恨 知 多 少,]
mon yō betsu kon chi ta sho
ask me separation sadness know much few
(If you) ask me how much I regret the parting. (much or little)

[luò huā chūn mù zhēng fēn fēn
落 花 春 暮 爭 紛 紛。]
raku kwa shun bō so fun fun
falling flowers spring end compete in (same)
with turmoil in confusion (mixed)
I would avow that my sorrow is as much as the falling flowers at the end of spring struggling with
one another in a tangle.

[yán yì bù kě jìn
言 亦 不 可 盡,]
gen eki fu ka jin
words also not possible (to express) all = (lit.) exhaust
Words cannot be exhausted

[qíng yì bù kě jí
情 亦 不 可 極。]
jo eki fu ka kioku
emotion also not possible to fathom ultimate = end
(lit.) depletes
Nor can the feeling be fathomed.

[hū   ér   cháng guì jiān cǐ   cí
呼   兒   長   跪   緘   此   辭,]
<u>ko</u>   <u>ja</u>   <u>cho</u> <u>ki</u>   <u>kan</u>   shi   <u>ji</u>
calling child sitting on   seal this words
      boy   one's knees   letter

So calling upon my son, I make him sit on the ground for a long time, and write to my dictation
these words (letter sealed is used for letter written)

[jì   jūn   qiān   lǐ   yáo   xiāng   yì
寄   君   千   里   遙   相   憶。]
<u>ki</u>   <u>kun</u>   <u>sen</u>   <u>ri</u>   <u>en</u>   <u>so</u>   <u>oku</u>
send to you thousand miles far   mutually think of =
                                          recollect

And, sending them to you over 1000 miles, we think of each other in (at a) distance.
                [Li Bai (701–762)]

107

[sòng yuán èr shǐ ān xī
送　元　二　使　安　西]

Genyi was going to Ansei as messenger, so author says their poetry.

[wèi chéng zhāo yǔ yì qīng chén
渭　城　朝　雨　浥　輕　塵,]
I   jo   cho   u   i   kei   jin
I castle morning rain wets light dust
The castle on the I river, i.e. a walled city

[kè   shè   qīng qīng liǔ sè   xīn
客　舍　青　青　柳　色　新。]
kaku sha   sei   sei   riu shiki shin
guest house blue blue willow color new
---inn---
In the inn where you will stay thereafter, the new color of the willow trees will be green green

[quàn jūn   gèng jìn   yī bēi jiǔ
勸　君　更　盡　一　杯　酒,]
kwan kun   ko   jin   iku hai shu
advise you lord newly annihilate one cup saki
I advise you, however, to put an end to a cup of wine

[xī   chū   yáng guān wú   gù   rén
西　出　陽　關　無　故　人。]
sei shutsu yo kwan mu   ko   jin
west departure Yo gate not original man
                barrier   old
Going westward through the Yo gate there will not be any old friend.

[By Wang Wei (699–761)]

[huáng hè lóu sòng mèng hào rán zhī guǎng líng
黄 鶴 樓 送 孟 浩 然 之 廣 陵]
ko   kaku ro so mo ko len shi ko   rio
yellow stork pavilion   --name--   going (to) -name of place-
              say goodbye of man   (name of land same as Yoshu)

[gù rén   xī   cí huáng hè   lóu
故 人   西 辭 黄 鶴   樓,]
ko-jin   sei ji ko kaku   ro
Old acquaintance west leave --------
An old acquaintance, starting from the west, takes leave of K.K.R.

[yān huā   sān yuè xià   yáng zhōu
煙 花   三 月 下   揚 州。]
en   kwa   san getsu ka   yo   shu
smoke flowers 3rd month go down -name of province-
In the month of March, when flowers (of blooming trees) are smoky (blurry) he descends (by
river) to Yoshu

[gū   fān yuǎn yǐng bì   kōng jìn
孤 帆 遠 影 碧 空 盡,]
ko   han en yei haki ku jin
solitary sail far shadow blue sky terminate
(I look from the storied house at the boat) the distant shade of the solitary sail is visible at the
very extreme of the blue sky.

[wéi jiàn cháng jiāng tiān jì   liú
唯 見 長 江 天 際 流。]
i   ken cho ko   ten sai riu
only see long Kiang heaven limit flow
              River
(and then moment after)

I only see the long River flowing into the horizon –horizon means approximation to Korio.
                         [By Li Bai (701–762)]

NOTES FOR "TAKING LEAVE OF A FRIEND"

[sòng yǒu rén

送　友　人]

So　Yu　Jin

Taking leave of a friend

[qīng shān héng běi guō

青　山　横　北　郭，]

sei　zan　o　hoku　kaku

blue　mt.　lie　north side of walled city.

　　　horizontally

Where blue mt. peaks are visible toward the northern suburb

[bái shuǐ rào dōng chéng

白　水　遶　東　城。]

haku　sui　gio　to　jo

white water encircle East castled town

And white water flows encircling the east of the city.

[cǐ dì yì wéi bié

此　地　一　為　別，]

shi　chi　ichi　i　betsu

This place once make separation

　　　ground

At this place we have for once to separate.

[gū péng wàn lǐ zhēng

孤　蓬¹⁵　萬　里　征。]

ko　ho　ban　ri　sei

solitary rootless 10000 miles go away

　　　plant

　　　dead grass

Like solitary dead grass (blown by northern wind) this departing one goes through 10000 miles

---

¹⁵ 孤蓬: Not dead grass but lone rootless plant.

IIO

[fú   yún   yóu zǐ   yì,
浮   雲   遊 子   意,]
<u>fu</u>   <u>wun</u>   <u>yu</u> <u>shi</u>   <u>i</u>
floating cloud –wanderer   mind
His (or your) mind may be that of a floating cloudlike wanderer.

[luò   rì   gù rén   qíng
落   日   故 人   情。]
<u>raku</u>   <u>jitsu</u>   <u>ko</u> <u>jin</u>   <u>jo</u>
Falling sun old acquaintance emotion
setting
(As for me) the sorrow of parting with an old acquaintance is comparable to the setting of the sun.

[huī   shǒu zì   zī   qù,
揮   手16 自   玆   去,]
<u>ki</u>   <u>shu</u> <u>ji</u>   <u>ji</u>   <u>kiō</u>
Shaking hands from this   away
Brandishing   place
Wringing hands in despairing resolution from this place it is away! (We have decided to separate)

[xiāo xiāo   bān   mǎ   míng
蕭 蕭   班   馬   鳴。]
"<u>sho</u> <u>sho</u>"   <u>han</u>   <u>ba</u>   <u>mei</u>
onomatopoeia for a separating horse neigh
solitary horse neighing
(We men have so decided) and yet our very horses separating, neigh sho sho.

[Li Bai (701–762)]

---

16 揮手: Waving clasped hands in front of the chest.

NOTES FOR "LEAVE-TAKING NEAR SHOKU"

[sòng   yǒu rén rù   shǔ
送   友 人   入   蜀]

so   yu jin   niu   shoku
Taking leave of a friend   entering Shoku

[jiàn shuō cán   cóng   lù
見   说   蠶   叢   路,]

ken   setsu san   so   ro
see   talk   silkworm groping ways
We hear it said that Sanso's roads (Sanso was old king of Shoku)
(wild silkworm in Shoku)

[qí   qū   bù   yì   xíng
崎   嶇   不   易   行。]

ki   ku   fu   i   ko
steepness of mts. not   easy go
Are steep and not easy to go

[shān cóng rén miàn qǐ
山   從 人   面   起,]

san   ju   jin   men   ki
mts. from man face   rise
because mts. rise up in the very face of a man

[yún   bàng   mǎ   tóu   shēng
雲   傍   馬   頭   生。]

wun   bo   ba   to   sei
clouds alongside horse head grow out
And clouds grow alongside the horse's head

[fāng shù   lǒng   qín   zhàn
芳   樹   籠   秦   棧,]

ho   ju   ro   shin   san
Fragrant trees cover up Shin Dynasty supported way (as mt. did)
(but at the same time) (this being spring time) fragrant woods must be covering us thru
supported paths of Shin

[chūn liú rào shǔ chéng
春 流 遶 蜀 城。]
shun riu gio Shoku jo
spring flow encircle Shoku city (castled)
And spring brooks meandering the Shuku city

[shēng chén yīng yǐ dìng
升 沈 應 已 定,]
sho chin o ki tei
rise sink ought already be settled
 -fortune-
Men's fates are already predetermined

[bù bì wèn jūn píng
不 必 問 君 平。]
fu hi mon kun pei
Not necessarily ask (Kun pei)
So that you have no need to ask Kunpei. (a famous old sage of Kunpei skilled in divination, who could be fortune teller in general.)

[By Li Bai (701–762)]

golden tomb

[dēng   jīn   líng   fèng huáng tái

登   金   陵   鳳   凰   臺]

to   kin   rio   ho   o   tai

Climb up Nan   Kin   phoenix   terrace

[fèng huáng tái   shàng fèng huáng yóu

鳳   凰   臺   上   鳳   凰   遊,]

ho   o   tai   jo   ho   o   yu

phoenix   terrace above phoenix   play

Above the ho terrace the hos used to play.

[fèng qù   tái   kōng jiāng zì   liú

鳳   去   臺   空   江   自   流。]

ho   kio   dai   ku   ko   ji   riu

phoenix away terrace vacant river of itself flow

The hos have fled, the terrace bare, the river flows away

                                   by itself alone

                                   (seen from above)

[wú   gōng huā cǎo mái yōu   jìng

吳   宮   花   草   埋   幽   徑,]

Go   kiu   kwa   so   mai   yu   kei

dynastic palace flower grass bury sombre path

 Go

Where the Go palace stood, flowers & grass bury up the somber path

[jìn   dài   yī   guān chéng gǔ   qiū

晉   代   衣   冠   成   古   丘。]

shin   dai   i   kwan   sei   ko   kiu

dynasty dynasty garment caps   become old hill

 Shin

Where the Shin dynasty courtiers have lived (clothes & caps)

the foundations of those houses have become old hills.

[sān shān bàn luò qīng tiān wài
三　山　半　落　青　天　外，]
san　zan　han　raku　sei　ten　gai
3　mts　half　fall　blue　heaven　outside
--name--
The triangle mt. is half disappearing beyond the blue sky

[èr shuǐ zhōng fēn bái lù zhōu
二　水　中　分　白　鷺　洲。]
ni　sui　chu　bun　haku　ro　shu
2　water　middle　divide　white　heron　island
　　　　　　-----name-----
And the white heron island divides the waters into two

[zǒng wéi fú yún néng bì rì
總　為　浮　雲　能　蔽　日，]
so　i　fu　wun　no　hei　jitsu
altogether　because　floating　clouds　well　cover　sun
　　　　　of
Because everywhere the floating clouds can fully cover up the sun.

[cháng ān bù jiàn shǐ rén chóu
長　安　不　見　使　人　愁。]
Cho　an　fu　ken　shi　jin　shu
-City Capital-　not　see　let　man　sorry
So Choan is invisible and makes men sad.

[By Li Bai (701–762)]

NOTES FOR "SOUTH-FOLK IN COLD COUNTRY"

[gǔfēng zhī liù

古 风 之 6]

Another Kofu 6th

[dài mǎ bù sī yuè

代 马 不 思 越,]

<u>Dai</u> <u>ba</u> <u>fu</u> <u>shi</u> <u>etsu</u>

place horse not think of Etsu

in north)   in the south

The horses of Dai, tho taken to Etsu, care nothing for Etsu

[yuè qín bù liàn yān

越 禽 不 懋 燕。]

<u>Etsu</u> <u>kin</u> <u>fu</u> <u>ren</u> <u>yen</u>

Etsu birds not love En - a north region

So the Etsu birds have no love for an alien En.

[qíng xìng yǒu suǒ xí

情 性 有 所 习,]

<u>jo</u> <u>sei</u> <u>yu</u> <u>sho</u> <u>shu</u>

emotion nature has that which habituated

                 is

Human emotions & natures are things that spring from habit

[tǔ fēng gù qí rán

土 风 固 其 然。]

<u>do</u> <u>fu</u> <u>kō</u> <u>ki</u> <u>zen</u>

local manners of that (ly) adj- ending

(earth) (wind) course ---so---

The powers which local manners have on one's mind are necessarily thus.

[xī　　bié　　yàn　　mén　　guān
昔　　别　　雁　　門　　關,]
seki　　betsu　　gan　　mon　　kan
(ancient) separate wild　gate　fort
former　　　　　　goose
yesterday　　　　　　---name of gate---
"Yesterday one has left the wild geese Tartars." (This is the Northern province of Dai. Why called wild geese? Because believed to come from north.)

[jīn　　shù　　lóng　　tíng　　qián
今　　戍　　龍　　庭　　前。]
kin　　jū　　riu　　tei　　zen
now garrison dragon yard before
　　(verb) --name of a locality—desert
"Today one has already come so far as the Dragon yard deserted front." (What sort of life do we lead here? is supplied)

[jīng　　shā　　luàn　　hǎi　　rì
驚　　沙　　亂　　海　　日,]
kei　　sha　　ran　　kaī　　jitsu
surprised desert turmoil sea　sun
　　　　sand-sea
"Sands surprised by wind cover in their turmoil the desert sea sun."

[fēi　　xuě　　mí　　hú　　tiān
飛　　雪　　迷[17]　　胡　　天。]
hi　　setsu　　mei　　kō　　ten
flying snow wanders　northern heaven
　　　　errs　barbarian
　　　　　　Tartar's
(When once winter comes) "The flying snow lets go astray the Manchurian heaven—one loses sight of the sky."

---

[17]　迷: Bewilders.

[jǐ   shī   shēng   hǔ   hé
蟣   蝨   生   虎   鶡,]
ki   shitsū   sei   kō   katsu
ants fleas grow on   tiger (a kind of bird famous for bravery)
antlike lice   (part of armor) fight till death.
(many)   soldiers wear their feathers on their helmets
                           ----on armor----
(Such life continuing for long) "Swarms of lice grow on the accountrments."

[xīn hún zhú jīng zhān
心   魂   逐   旌   旃。]
shin   kon   chiku   sei   sen
mind spirit drive banners banner made
                   made of   of silk
                   feathers
(And yet under such difficulty) Can one's mind be easy? No! "Because our mind and spirit must
drive upon (keep close attention to) the motion of the banners."

[kǔ zhàn gōng bù shǎng
苦 戰   功   不   賞,]
ku sen ko fū sho
hard fight merit not reward
Although one fights so hard, his merit is not rewarded. (The whole intent of this is that to let
soldiers undergo such distant hardship is inhuman for an Emperor.)

[zhōng chéng nán   kě xuān
忠   誠   難   可   宣。]
chu   sei   nan   ka   sen
loyalty faith difficult to   tell-express
(as one is not a horse or a bird) so if one were allowed to express all he feels of loyalty & faith he
would be satisfied.
"There is no chance to express one's loyalty and faith."

[shuí lián lǐ fēi   jiāng
誰 憐   李   飛   將,]
sui   ren   ri   hi   sho
who will be (general) flying general
     sorry for Ri   of quick motion

Who was sorry for flying general Ri. (History: in Kan Dynasty was famous Ri Shogun [General Li Guang] who fought more than 74 battles with the northern barbarians who called him the Flying Shugun. So skillful, he was contantly sent out for some expedition, and was never recalled—so he died in old age in one of the border battles.)

[bái   shǒu   mò   sān   biān
白   首   没   三   邊。]

<u>haku</u> <u>shū</u> <u>metsu</u> <u>san</u> <u>ben</u>
white head lost   thru outside provinces
                          outskirt
                          border regions

Ri[haku] is expressing the soldier's feelings. "The fate of Ri Shogun is probably mine too." "Whose white head was lost (died) in the three frontiers." Who died in old age. "Who will be sorry for me, in the fate of Rishogun?"

[By Li Bai (701–762)]

NOTES FOR "SENNIN POEM BY KAKUHAKU"

[yóu xiān shī]

游　仙　詩[18]

[fěi　　cuì　　　xì　　lán　　tiáo]

翡　　翠　　　戲　　蘭　　苕

hi　　sui　　　gi　　raw　　cho

red bird　green bird　play　orchid　clover or a kind of pea
　a kind of kingfisher

Red and green Kingfishers play among the orchids and clovers.

[róng　　sè　　gēng　　　xiāng　　xiān]

容　　　色　　更　　　　相　　　鮮

yo　　　shoku　ko　　　　sho　　　sen

appearance color　interchanging each other　fresh

Their appearances are more fresh by reflecting with each other.

[lǜ　　luó　　jié　　gāo　　lín]

綠　　蘿　　结　　高　　林

roku　ra　　ketsu　ko　　rin

green　vine　hang　high　forest

Green vines hang on and twine the high forest.

[méng　lóng　　gài　　　　yī　　shān]

蒙　　籠　　　蓋　　　　一　　山

mo　　ro　　　gai　　　　ichi　zan

to wear on　to put into　cover　one　mountain
the head　　basket
to cover
　obscure, dim

Darkly they cover the whole mountain.

---

[18] 游仙詩: "Wandering as an Immortal," a series of nineteen poems by Guo Pu (276–324). This is no. 3.

[zhōng yǒu míng jì shì]
中　　有　　冥　　寂　　士
chū yū mei seki shi
in it (there) is silent solitary man
In it there is a silent and solitary man.

[jìng xiào fǔ qīng xián]
静　　嘯　　撫　　清　　弦
sei sho bu sei gen
calmly sigh pat clear string (kin)
　　　(with pride)
　　(when a tiger cries, this is used)
Calmly he sighs and pats on the pure strings.

[fàng qíng líng xiāo wài]
放　　情　　凌　　霄　　外
ho jo ryo sho gai
to throw feeling rise up sky beyond
freeing heart
Freeing his heart, it rises up beyond the sky.

[jiáo ruǐ yì fēi quán]
嚼　蘂　　把　飛　泉
shaku zui yū hi sen
biting pistil of a flower dip up spouting fountain
Biting the flower pistils, he dips up spouting fountain.

[chì sōng lín shàng yóu]
赤　　松　　臨　　上　　游
seki sho rin jo yu
red pine looking on wander
The god of rain in the　　play
time of the Emperor Shinno
Ode makes the Stone Chamber of Seiōbo in Konron Mountain
Red pine plays (on the sky) looking down on him.

[jià   hóng   chéng   zǐ   yān]
驾   鴻   乘   紫   煙
ga   ko   jo   shi   yen

making carriage (perhaps a   ride   purple smoke
riding   kind of swan)

Making "ko" his carriage, he rides on purple, smoke.

                         refers to the god of rain.

[zuǒ   yì   fú   qiū   xiù]
左   把   浮   丘   袖
sa   yu   fu   kyu   shu

left to take (up) floating hill   sleeves

           name of a "sennin" in Sūkō mountain.

On the left, he takes the sleeve of Floating Hill
        the god

[yòu   pāi   hóng   yá   jiān]
右   拍   洪   崖   肩
wu   haku   ko   gai   ken

right to pat, to lay water rushing overhanging shoulder
     the hand on, as in a torrent   cliff
       a good humour name of a   a sheer side
                 "sennin"   of a hill,
                             a cliff, a
                     precipice over rocks

On the right, he (the god) pats on the shoulder of Water Cliff.

[jiè   wèn   fú   yóu   bèi]
借   問   蜉   蝣   輩
sha   mon   fu   yu   hai

temporarily ask bu Jap.   crowd (in contempt)
               a gnat, which is born
               in the morning
               & dies in the evening

Let me just try to ask you, oh! crowds of gnats!

[níng   zhī   guī   hè   nián]
寧   知   龜   鶴   年
Nei   chi   ki   kaku   nen
how   know   turtle   stork   age

How can you know the age of turtles and storks (which live for a thousand and ten thousand years)?

[By Guo Pu (276–324)]

NOTES FOR "A BALLAD OF THE MULBERRY ROAD"

[mò shàng sāng]
陌 上 桑[19]
<u>Hoku</u> <u>jo</u> <u>so</u>
Highway on mulberry tree

[rì chū dōng nán yú]
日 出 東 南 隅
<u>richi</u> <u>shatsu</u> <u>to</u> <u>nan</u> <u>gu</u>   Mr. Mori says that
sun rises East South corner   the lines are specially
The sun rises on the south east corner   beautiful

[zhào wǒ qín shì lóu]
照 我 秦 氏 樓
<u>sho</u> <u>ga</u> <u>shin</u> <u>shi</u> <u>ro</u>
shines (on) our name of a family two storied house
family clan
and it shines on the villa of the Shin clan.

[qín shì yǒu hǎo nǚ]
秦 氏 有 好 女
<u>Shin</u> <u>shi</u> <u>yu</u> <u>ko</u> <u>jō</u>
Shin family has pretty girl
The Shin family has a pretty daughter.

[zì míng wéi luó fū]
自 名 為 羅 敷
<u>ji</u> <u>mei</u> <u>i</u> <u>ra</u> <u>fu</u>
herself name make --girl's name--
She herself made her name gauze girl.

[luó fū shàn cán sāng]
羅 敷 善 蠶 桑
<u>ra</u> <u>fu</u> <u>zen</u> <u>san</u> <u>sō</u>
--Rafu-- excel in silkworm mulberry
Gauze girl was skillful in breeding mulberries to silkworm.

---

[19] The original has fifty-three lines of which Pound has translated the first fourteen lines.

[cǎi　sāng　　chéng　nán　yú]
採　　桑　　　城　　南　　隅

sai　so　　　jo　　nan　gu

pluck　mulberry　castle　south　corner

She plucks mulberry leaves at the south corner of the castle.

[qīng　sī　wéi　lóng　xì]
青　　絲　　為　　籠　　系

sei　shi　i　　ro　　kei

green　strings　make　basket　warp
blue

She makes these strings the warp of her basket. (wears them in)

[guì　zhī　wéi　lóng　gōu]
桂　　枝　　為　　籠　　鉤

kei　shi　i　　ro　　kō

Katsura branch　makes　basket　shoulder strings
　　　　　　　　　　　　　　　strings to fasten around the 2 shoulders

She makes the shoulder straps of her basket out of very baskets.

[tóu　shàng　wō　dùo　jì]
頭　　上　　倭　　墮　　髻

to　　jo　　wa　　da　　kei

head　on　to curl　incline　hair arrangement (maze)
　　　　　　like a snake to one side

On her head is coiled a special arrangement of a girl's hair that falls over left side—tress-arrangement

[ěr　zhōng　míng　yuè　zhū]
耳　　中　　明　　月　　珠

ji　　chu　　mei　getsu　shū

ear　in　bright　moon　gem
　　　　　---mean pearls---

In her ear shine moon gems.

125

[xiāng qǐ wéi xià qún]
緗[20]   綺   為   下   裙

sho   ki   i   ka   kiō

light green special wool   makes under skirt
            from some kind
            of cotton cloth

Light green name of cloth she makes or uses for her under skirt.

[zǐ qǐ wéi shàng rú]
紫   綺   為   上   襦

shi   ki   i   jo   jū

purple some kind makes upper vest.
      of cloth

purple she uses for her over-vest

[xíng zhě jiàn luó fū]
行 者   見   羅   敷

ko   sha   ken ra   fū

go   one who sees Rafu

Those who pass by seeing

[xià dān lǚ zī xū]
下   擔   捋   髭   鬚

ka   tan   ratsu shi   shū

taking down burden twist   the upper lip mustache

put down their load and pull the mustache on their upper lip.

[From *Ballads of the Han* (2nd-1st centuries B.C.)]

---

[20] 緗: Light yellow (silk).

NOTES FOR "OLD IDEA OF CHOAN BY ROSORIU"

[cháng ān gǔ yì
長　安　古　意²¹]
"Old Idea of Choan"

by poetical courtesy the poet pretends that he is speaking of the Choan of Kan Days, making allusions to Yoshin [Yang Xiong], a Kan retired gentleman at the end.

[cháng ān dà dào lián　　　xiá xié
長　安　大　道　連　　　　狹斜,]
Cho- an big road continuous with narrow streets (no verb).
Choan's broad avenues
This first line contains theme or germ of the whole.

[qīng niú bái mǎ qī xiāng chē
青　牛　白　馬　七　香　車。]
blue cow, white horse, seven fragrant carriage.
　　　　　　　　woods (wheeled)
　　　　　　　　incense
Cows are drawing these chariots made of fragrant wood.
blue cow is for carriage, white horse for riders.

[yù niǎn zòng héng guò zhǔ dì
玉　輦　縱　橫　過　主　第,]
jewel palanquins longitudinally horizontally pass prince's mansion.
　(by hand　----crossing----　　　before　Yashiki)

[jīn biān luò yì xiàng hóu jiā
金　鞭　絡　繹　向　侯　家。]
Gold saddle weaving unraveling toward marquis' house
golden saddles in

---

²¹ The original has sixty-eight lines of which Fenollosa has presented the first sixteen lines.

[lóng   xián   bǎo   gài   chéng zhāo   rì
龍　　銜　　寶　　蓋　　承　　朝　　日，]
Dragon swallow precious canopy receive morning sun
Dragon munching costly (sunshade)
means the dragon on top of the handle
The precious canopy which the dragon swallows

[fèng   tǔ   liú   sū   dài   wǎn   xiá
風　　吐　　流　　蘇　　帶　　晚　　霞。]
Hos vomit flowing tassel imbibe evening fog
    emit shaking (of saddle)
lacquerer or cauldron on the saddle are belted by the evening haze.
The flowing tassels which the Hos vomit

[bǎi   zhàng yóu   sī   zhēng rào   shù
百　　丈　　遊　　絲　　爭　　繞　　樹，]
Hundred jo floating threads vying intertwine trees
    (10 feet)   to twist about (in garden)
For a thousand feet   with thread
Mr. Mori thinks it means the ripples of air which alone the outsider could see as sign of many
gathered together, but it seems to me a vista.

[yī   qún   jiāo   niǎo   gòng   tí   huā
一　　羣　　嬌　　鳥　　共　　啼　　花。]
one group coquetting birds together warble flowers
 a flock   vain   mutually chirp to the flowers
Mr. Mori thinks it is women in garden as heard from outside.
End of 1st stanza

[tí   huā   xì   dié   qiān   mén   cè
啼　　花　　戲　　蝶　　千　　門　　側，]
Warbling flowers, playing butterflies thousand gate side.
Birds understood as butterflies playing with the flowers, are seen by the side of the thousand
gates. (as seen from the streets.)

[bì   shù   yín   tái   wàn   zhŏng sè
碧   樹   銀   臺   萬   種   色。]
White jewel trees silver platforms myriad kinds colors
jade   terrace   seed
        in gardens seen above fences
    both are of myriad kinds of colors
      color may be double, fragrance of trees, hues of buildings

[fù   dào   jiāo   chuāng   zuò   hé   huān
複   道   交   窗   作   合   歡,]
covered roads interchanging window-holes make meeting pleasure
(corridors)   regularly interweave   mutual
           at various heights   that is, as they circle around the mansion
         or maybe interlacing   they can see one another from indoors.
                Seem to be a name for form of windows.

[shuāng què   lián   méng chuí   fèng yì
雙   闕   連   甍   垂   鳳   翼。]
Double towers continue tile   hang-down ho   wings
      towers in row tiles made in form of birds along the edge

[liáng jiā   huà   gé   tiān   zhōng qǐ
梁   家   畫   閣   天   中   起,]
Rio's   house painted stories heaven middle stand
Some family name
Rioki a general of Kan
Rio means <u>beam</u>

[hàn dì   jīn   jīng yún wài   zhí
漢   帝   金   莖   雲   外   直。]
Kan emperor golden stalk cloud beyond erect
Butei of Kan had a high golden lotus made to collect dew, a sennin idea
    These things said to have still existed in To.
     erects itself even higher than the clouds.

[lóu   qián xiāng   wàng bù xiāng   zhī

樓   前   相   望   不   相   知,]

Building front mutually seeing not mutually knowing

In front of building (people) see one another but do not know.

[mò   shàng xiāng   féng   jù   xiāng   shí

陌   上   相   逢   詎   相   識。]

Footpath on   mutually meeting but how mutually knowing

Sidewalks   people   why   acquainted

                 of course they do not

    End of 2d stanza

                          [By Lu Zhaolin (636–689)]

from "To-Em mei Shu," Works of Toemmei

Both prose & poetry

[tíng yún

停 雲]

"Teiwun" <u>Fixed</u> (not moving) <u>Cloud</u>

The subject of 4 connected poems

1ˢᵗ

[ăi	ăi	tíng	yún	méng	méng	shí	yŭ
靉	靉	停	雲,	濛	濛	時	雨。]
<u>ai</u>	<u>ai</u>	<u>tei</u>	<u>wun</u>,	<u>mo</u>	<u>mo</u>	<u>ji</u>	<u>u</u>

gathering gathering fixed clouds, pattering pattering temporary rain.

The fixed clouds gather & gather, and the intermittent showers patter & patter.

[bā	biăo	tóng	hūn
八	表	同	昏,]
<u>hachi</u>	<u>hiō</u>	<u>dō</u>	<u>kon</u>

eight surface same dark

The earth in all directions is equally dark.

[píng	lù	yī	zŭ
平	路	伊	阻。²²]
<u>hei</u>	<u>rō</u>	<u>ī</u>	<u>lan</u>

flat road this wide & flat

The level road stretches out into the flat distance

[jìng	jì	dōng	xuān
靜	寄	東	軒,]
<u>sei</u>	<u>ki</u>	<u>to</u>	<u>ken</u>

calmly remain east room

I remain quiet in my Eastern room

---

²² 阻: Troublesome.

[chūn   láo   dú   fǔ
春   醪   獨   撫。]
<u>shun</u>   <u>ko</u>   <u>doku</u>   <u>hī</u>
spring   home made   alone   stroke
         sake
Solitary I stroke my spring home-made brew.

[liáng   péng   yōu   miǎo
良   朋   悠   邈]
<u>rio</u>   <u>ho</u>   <u>yu</u>   <u>bo</u>
good   friend   distant
My good friends have grown strange or are far away

[sāo   shǒu   yán   zhù
搔   首   延   佇]
<u>so</u>   <u>shu</u>   <u>yen</u>   <u>tei</u>
droop   head   long   stand still.
Drooping my head, I stand still for a long time.

2ND

[tíng   yún   ǎi   ǎi
停   雲   靄   靄,]
<u>tei</u>   <u>wun</u>   <u>ai</u>   <u>ai</u>
   (same as before)

[shí   yǔ   méng   méng
時   雨   濛   濛。]
<u>ji</u>   <u>u</u>   <u>mo</u>   <u>mo</u>
   (same as before)

[bā   biǎo   tóng   hūn
八   表   同   昏,]
<u>hap</u>   <u>hio</u>   <u>do</u>   <u>kon</u>
   (same as before)

[píng lù chéng jiāng
平 陵 成 江。]
hei riku sei ko
flat land becomes river.
The flat land becomes a river.

[yǒu jiǔ yǒu jiǔ
有 酒 有 酒,]
yu shū yu shū
is sake is sake
Here is wine! here is wine!

[xián yǐn dōng chuāng
閑 飲 東 窗。]
kan in to so
at leisure drink East window
Leisurely I drink at my Eastern window.

[yuàn yán huái rén
願 言 懷 人,]
gwan gen kwai jin
(wish) speak think of man
hoping (word)
Longing for words, I think of man.

[zhōu chē mǐ cóng
舟 車 靡 從。]
shu sha bi ju
ship carriage not follow
Alas, no ship or carriage attends me.

3ᵈ

[dōng yuán zhī shù
東 園 之 樹,]
tō yen shi ju
east garden of tree
On the trees of my Eastern garden

[zhī   tiáo   zài   róng
枝   條   載²³   榮。]
shi   jō   sai   yei
branch twig again flourish
boughs and sprays are again luxuriant;

[jìng yòng xīn   hǎo
競   用   新   好,]
kio   yo   shin ko
race use   new   good
and vying to make the most of their new beauty

[yǐ   zhāo yú   qíng
以   招   余   情。]
i   sho   yo   jo
with invite my   passion
will they appeal to my affection.

[rén yì   yǒu   yán
人   亦   有   言,]
jin shaku yu   gen
man again is   speak
Men often are saying

[rì   yuè   yú   zhēng
日   月   於   征。]
jitsu getsu kan   sei
sun moon have turn
That sun and moon have their turning.

[ān   dé   cù   xí
安   得   促   席,]
an   tōku soku seki
tranquil get place seat
Sitting my mat where I can be at ease

---

²³ 載: Begin (to).

[shuō   bǐ   píng   shēng
說   彼   平   生?[24]]
setsu   hi   hei   sei
to be glad his   flat   born
              its   natural or customary
Let me take joy in the cause of nature.

4th

[piān   piān   fēi   niǎo
翩   翩   飛   鳥,]
hen   hen   hī   chō
many wings many wings flying bird
Fluttering, fluttering, the birds that fly

[xī   wǒ   tíng   kē
息   我   庭   柯。]
soku ga   tei   ka
rest my   garden tree (solitary life)
Come to rest on the love tree in my yard.

[liǎn   hé   xián   zhǐ
斂   翮   閑   止,]
ren   hen   kan   shi
folding wings quietly stop
Folding their wings they perch quiet,

[hǎo   shēng   xiāng   hè
好   聲   相   和。]
ko   sei   so   wa
good   voice   each other to be familier
lovely
And with sweet voice they speak thus with each other.

---

[24] 安得促席, /说彼平生?: How to sit face to face with you, / to talk about our aspirations and interests?

[qǐ   wú   tā   rén
豈   無   他   人,]
gai   mu   ta   nin
(negative) not   other man
It is not that there is no other man than he

[niàn   zǐ   shí   duō
念   子   實   多。]
nen   shi   shoku   ta
think of you truly much
love
but we love him the most of all.

[yuàn yán bù   huò
願   言   不   獲,]
gwan gen fu   kaku
wish speak not reach
Since our longing to speak to him cannot reach him,

[bào   hèn   rú hé
抱   恨   如 何!]
ho   kon   jō ka
to bear in mind deep sorrow like what
We hold deep sorrow in our mind, but cannot help it!!

[By Tao Yuanming (365–427)]

136